Offstage Voices

LINESET # 45
TRIM @+ 24'-6"

LINESET # 41
TRIM @+ 28'-9"

LINESET # 36
TRIM @+ 28'-6"

LINESET # 28
TRIM @+ 30'-0"

LINESET # 15
TRIM @+ 26'-6"

LINESET # 15
TRIM @+ 26'-6"

LINESET # 7
TRIM @+ 26'

FOG

FOG

#1 Catwalk

Left Proscenium Ladder

Right Proscenium Ladder

Permanent #1 Catwalk Position

Stage Left Box 1 & 2

Current position Of added lighting Pipe under
1 Catwalk

Stage Right Box 1 & 2

Balcony Rail

NOT SHOWN
IN CORRECT
POSITION

Stage Left Box 3 & 4

SR Side Catwalk

Up

Stage Right Box 3 & 4

Balcony Rail-1

SR Side Catwalk

#2 Catwalk

Stage

#2 Catwalk Overhung

NOT SHOWN IN
CORRECT POSITION

NIUM LADDER
d View

Catwalk

structions in this section from House Lights

#3 Catwalk

e Light Ladder

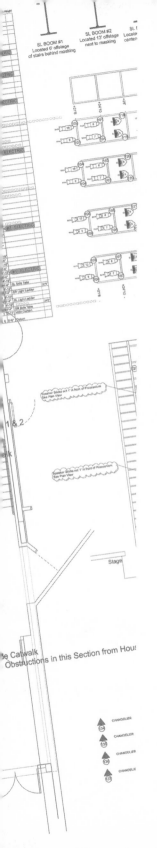

Offstage Voices

Life in Twin Cities Theater

Peg Guilfoyle

Foreword by Sally Wingert

MINNESOTA
HISTORICAL
SOCIETY PRESS

The publication of the book was funded in part by the Elmer L. and Eleanor Andersen Publications Fund.

www.mnhspress.org
The Minnesota Historical Society Press is a member of the Association of American University Presses.

Manufactured in the United States of America
10 9 8 7 6 5 4 3 2 1

♾ The paper used in this publication meets the minimum requirements of the American National Standard for Information Sciences—Permanence for Printed Library Materials, ANSI Z39.48-1984.

International Standard Book Number
ISBN: 978-0-87351-970-0 (paper)
ISBN: 978-0-87351-971-7 (e-book)

Library of Congress Cataloging-in-Publication Data

Guilfoyle, Peg, 1960–
Offstage voices : life in Twin Cities theater / Peg Guilfoyle ; foreword by Sally Wingert.
    pages   cm
Includes index.
    ISBN 978-0-87351-970-0 (paperback) — ISBN 978-0-87351-971-7 (ebook)
    1. Theater—Minnesota—Minneapolis—History—20th century. 2. Theater—Minnesota—St. Paul—History—20th century. I. Title.
    PN2277.M54G85   2015
    792.09776'5790904—dc23

                                                                        2015019902

This and other Minnesota Historical Society Press books are available from popular e-book vendors.

Book design by Wendy Holdman

Contents

Foreword

by Sally Wingert

Shh, let's just keep this to ourselves.

As an actor in the Twin Cities, I live somewhere between pride and fear.

Pride, that our cities support a vibrant, truly progressive theater scene. This is a community that encourages new work, companies large and small, challenging ideas, and innovative productions by financially enabling the work and, as importantly, actually seeing it.

Fear, that our theater scene will become "known" to the rest of the country and we will be inundated with actors moving here to make the kind of careers they had always hoped to have.

Actor Sally Wingert. (Photo courtesy of Sally Wingert)

Selfish? Possibly.

Our Twin Cities are enviable places to be a theater artist, as *Offstage Voices* makes abundantly clear. Here it is possible to be an actor and a parent, a director and a homeowner, a set designer and a community organizer—all while doing our theater work at a very high level. We live here and thrive because theater is more than a once-a-year event for our audiences. It has become a necessary part of their cultural landscape.

There's something in this book for everyone—the audience, the practitioners, educators, young people considering a life in the theater, their parents. The voices here come from every corner of our community—playwrights, producers, directors, designers, and performers—talking about the excitement, the joy, and the deep satisfaction a life in the theater gives them. These voices—which I hear in person, every day in my work, both on stage and off—have plenty to say, both insightful and cautionary. In the thick of rehearsing and performing, it's hard to talk about the how and why of what we do or to grab time with our friends to anecdotally discuss the work. *Offstage Voices* allows me to listen in on those stories and at the same time lets our audiences get to know us a little more personally.

The theater world changes constantly, morphing as artistic minds respond to our world, the cultural landscape, the next new thought. There's a healthy climate here that encourages theaters to emerge and, sometimes, be dismantled. I could not have guessed, almost forty years ago, what the face of Twin Cities theater would look like today. I was graduating from high school in a near-western suburb, seeing shows at the Cricket, Dudley Riggs's Brave New Workshop, and the Guthrie, among other places. I was about to dip my toe into the scene and audition for roles at theaters that are now no more than a memory. What began as a toe dip turned into a lifelong swim, a true love affair for me, and a sustaining career.

The first time I remember seeing Peg Guilfoyle, she was wrangling a live horse on the Guthrie stage for a production of *Cyrano de Bergerac*. The duties of a production stage manager are wide ranging, including figuring out how the young actors with brooms and buckets could keep close enough to Dolly so if the mare felt an urge they could respond, quickly. In her time as Guthrie production manager, and at other theaters, Peg capably wrangled many actors, directors, shows, and entire seasons.

Peg has been a friend and cohort since 1985; her depth of experience and profound love of the theater make this book an insider's guide to the hows and whys of our local theater world. She has asked us about our lives in the theater, allowed us to recall the past and muse about what's next.

In the answers, *Offstage Voices* captures the pulse and temperature of our theater world as it stands right here, right now. It's a portrait of the people who make it happen, in their own words. They tell it like it is with candor and humor.

You'll find personal truths about the state of our theater scene: how it came about and how it might evolve in the future, what it's like to live and work in the Twin Cities. You'll find the answers to questions, both pragmatic and poetic, about how theater is made. Want to know how a play gets written and finds a home on area stages? How an artistic director begins selecting a season? Or how people have gotten their start in the theater? The answers are here.

And you'll find some answers to the question "why?" These discussions are ones I'd like to have with my compatriots, if we only had time.

I'm an actor, living in St. Paul. This is my community. These are the stories, recollections, and dreams of my colleagues, speaking from offstage and deep in the heartbeat of theater life.

Enjoy. I'm off to rehearsal.

Acknowledgments

I am deeply grateful to the offstage voices who sat with me as I prepared this book. It was a treat and a thrill to step outside the daily hurly-burly of the theater and talk about why and how this work is done.

Great gratitude to Lou Bellamy, Sarah Bellamy, Sonya Berlovitz, Bain Boehlke, Michael Brindisi, Peter Brosius, Carlyle Brown, Chris Code, Jesse Cogswell, Jeremy Cohen, Richard Cohen, Richard Cook, Marcus Dilliard, Teresa Eyring, Barbara Field, Nathaniel Fuller, Bradley Greenwald, Rich Hamson, H. Adam Harris, Michelle Hensley, Alberto Justiniano, Aditi Kapil, Kevin Kling, Wendy Knox, Jeff Larson, C. Andrew Mayer, Tyler Michaels, John Miller-Stephany, Bonnie Morris, Dipankar Mukherjee, Kira Obolensky, Ron Peluso, T. Mychael Rambo, Jack Reuler, Randy Reyes, Michael Robins, Peter Rothstein, Joel Sass, Rick Shiomi, Anna Sundberg, Kate Sutton-Johnson, Christine Tschida, Ricardo Vazquez, and Sally Wingert. I also had a stirring group conversation with students from the 2014 Minnesota Centennial Showboat production: Bear Brummel, Katherine Fried, Jane Heer, Kelsey Peterjohn, and Daniel Piering, all from the University of Minnesota/Guthrie Theater BFA Actor Training Program. Jeffrey Hatcher gave permission to quote materials from his play *Jeffrey Hatcher's Hamlet*. I have retold a few stories here from my own *The Guthrie Theater: Images, History, and Inside Stories* (Nodin Press, 2006), and added many more.

We are fortunate to have so many significant voices in the theater community, but one result of that wealth is that it's not been possible to include them all here. Similarly, not every form of theater is represented.

I asked the people I interviewed to send me their favorite images of themselves at work; many thanks to the photographers who allowed use of their photos here. I wish there had been room for more. Photo captions include credits for the voices in this book; all directors and designers are credited on pages 199–200.

Interviews have been edited for clarity and space. All these conversations were transcribed by a hardy band of volunteers: notably Mary Benner, plus Dana Morison, Maria Moncur, and Maggie Baillie. Maggie Baillie also acted as editorial assistant for this project, which was a gift and a pleasure.

Portions of the manuscript were read at various stages by Tamra Anderson, Lou Bellamy, Jeremy Cohen, Dave Kenney, Charlotte Preston, Sally Wingert, and Sara Wright. Clinton Little kept my laptop system running, and many of the interviews were done in the big-windowed workspace at Kellogg Square in downtown St. Paul. I read the extremely useful Minnesota Playlist website regularly while writing this book, and relied on, and enjoyed, Frank Whiting's book *Minnesota Theatre: From Old Fort Snelling to the Guthrie*. Many people in the theater community helped with bits of information and connection as I stitched it all together: thank you.

Thanks to Pamela McClanahan, director of the Minnesota Historical Society Press, for her interest in developing this project and editors Josh Leventhal and Shannon Pennefeather for their guidance.

I'm grateful as always to my husband John Baillie, daughter Maggie, son John, and his Anna Novikova. Also to longtime colleague and dear friend Sheila Livingston.

But my deepest gratitude, my thankfulness, belongs to the theater colleagues with whom I've been privileged to work and laugh and wonder over the years in the theater. Some of you are in these pages, and some are not. We are lucky to work in the arts; that's what this book is about.

Offstage Voices

Introduction

I am an unabashed romantic about the theater. I thrill to the necessarily collective nature of the enterprise and its complete dependence on the humanity of its practitioners. I think of current practitioners as the direct lineal descendants of the players of the nineteenth-century stock companies; the Elizabethan rogues and vagabonds; the masked ones perched on their tall footwear—their cothurni—whispering to the back rows of the Greek stadia; all the way back to some furry and befurred creature, eyes gleaming, who stepped up to the firelight to enthrall the tribe. I believe the actor who pauses before he speaks "to be or not to be" is trailed by a long and ghostly line of predecessors who have climbed that mountain before him and who gather in the shadows of the house and backstage to hear the speech delivered again.

I believe that empty theaters are inhabited and that's why there is a "ghost light" on dark stages. I like old backdrops and painted scenery, antique stagecraft tricks that still work, and the sight of a group of stagehands pushing wagons of scenery. I like young actors with chops, and seasoned ones who command an audience with a silent turn of the head, or those who can lead a laugh all the way around a thrust stage just by turning their bodies. And I like being astonished by the constant reinvention of our craft and by the speculation about how it will remake itself in the future.

I also love to see an audience come out into the lobbies, clutching their programs and talking. I eavesdrop without shame.

This does not mean that I am foolish about the theater; years of work in the business prevent starry eyes. I do not suffer from the common misperception that the theater is a "family," unless we add a modifier, such as "not necessarily healthy." I no longer believe first rehearsal speeches that say "our show is better than anything in New York right now." I have a practiced set of eyes, the result of years of work as a stage manager and production manager. I can see a costume with a sagging hem, the shadow of an actor in the wings at the wrong moment, a rushed light cue or a missed one, a moment's uncertainty in a young actor. I know that any artistic endeavor has a stunningly large failure rate; it is a perilous profession.

None of these qualities prevent me from catching my breath as the houselights go down and the stage lights go up; from willingly dropping the world outside and wholeheartedly entering the world of the play, the world made especially for me and others in the audience. They do not prevent my heart from soaring during the bows, after which I am one of those clutching my program and talking as I exit. There is always, without fail, something worth watching and talking about in the theater.

This book is about theater work—how these apparent acts of prestidigitation happen—and, in particular, the theaters of the Twin Cities of St. Paul and Minneapolis. The theater community here is as much a part of the landscape as the Mississippi River and the high blue midwestern sky. What are the elements that have allowed it to thrive? To become so strongly embedded, so well supported by the citizenry, and so properly celebrated? Why have theater people been attracted to move here, stay here, and become part of the creative web?

Some aspects of Twin Cities and Minnesota culture are well known, even axiomatic: a well-educated populace, strong civic engagement, heartland values of responsibility and work ethic, the Land of 10,000 Lakes, the great north woods. And some sweeping generalizations about the Midwest and Minnesota are less kindly: stolid inhabitants, inhospitable climate, a certain homogeneity, and the apparently durable moniker "flyover land."

Stereotypes become stereotypes because they contain grains of truth, sufficient to appear at first glance as a solid construction. It is useful sometimes to flip them in order to consider them. Stolid equals not flighty. Inhospitable climate translates as weather extremes sufficient to discourage the weak-hearted from moving here. Homogenous . . . happily, we're moving away from that, along with the rest of the world, although plenty of work remains to be done. Flyover land? Not for the millions of us who live here, many of whom use the phrase *Upper Midwest*—to distinguish us from Iowa, I suppose—and some of whom are starting to call us the capitol of the North. Sounds better. More hip.

Well-educated populace. Well, we are. Strong civic engagement? Our U.S. Senator Al Franken (a former *Saturday Night Live* cast member) says, "I grew up in Minnesota, where we treasure our tradition of civic engagement—and our record of having the nation's highest voter participation." Land of 10,000 Lakes? Self-explanatory—though, in fact, we have more than ten thousand. A number of these lakes are in the Twin Cities metro proper, and that is not even to speak of the mighty Mississippi River that winds right through its heart. Think a large metropolitan area studded with beaches, parks, and woodlands.

Minneapolis writer Carol Becker characterized Minnesotans well in her opinion piece in the *Star Tribune* in December 2014:

> We are the smart kid who everyone wanted to copy off of in math class. . . . We were never going to be picked as the one most likely to succeed (New York), as the hardest partyer (New Orleans), or as the suave guy who could dance (Miami), or as the duuude (Los Angeles). We're the one who made parents say: "They are so nice! Why don't you hang out with *them* more?"
>
> We bowl more, bike more, buy fewer Barbies and join zombie hordes more. If you are a national company, you want to come here, because we educate our kids, stay late and get our work done, no matter how menial or stupid the job. Because it is the right thing to do. We are Minnesota Nice. Get over it.

We also love the arts in Minnesota, theater included. According to the Minnesota State Arts Board—an admittedly partisan perspective—67 percent of Minnesotans have attended an arts activity within the past year; 60 percent of Minnesotans are involved in the arts by doing some creative activity in their daily lives; and 95 percent of Minnesotans believe the arts are an important or essential part of the overall education of Minnesota children. In 2014, *Places Rated Almanac* ranked the Twin Cities eighth out of 354 metropolitan areas in the United States and Canada for its variety of and participation in the arts.

An oft-repeated but difficult-to-confirm axiom is that the Twin Cities are second only to New York in something called "theater seats per capita" (or "theater activity," or "as a center of theater"), a claim that has been appearing in print (with that same caveat) since at least 1969, when no less a publication than New York City's *Village Voice* called Minneapolis "America's second theatre city after New York." A more recent, and more quantifiable, measure comes from the 2013 Minneapolis Creative Vitality Index (CVI), a report produced by the City of Minneapolis but underlain by a statistic tagged to the "entire Minneapolis–St. Paul–Bloomington Metropolitan Statistical Area, aka Metro Minnesota." The metro CVI is the fifth-highest reported, topped only by Washington, DC; New York; Los Angeles; and Boston. The CVI, according to the report, "measures annual changes in the economic health of highly creative industries using information about organizational revenue, jobs, and other measures from creative businesses and nonprofits." And again, "by measuring the share of creative jobs, arts spending, and creative for-profit and nonprofit organizations in a given city or region, the CVI captures nuances of the creative sector that many other measures miss."

Among the nuances referred to, and reported on by Jon Spayde in *The Line* newsletter in May 2013, is that the Minneapolis creative sector contributes about $700 million annually into the economy, with that figure rising to $831 million in the 2014 update, and employs close to 20,000 Minneapolitans, constituting five percent of the city's jobs. The per capita rate of revenue for theater companies in Minneapolis is fourteen times the national average. The rates of revenue and charitable giving to all kinds of arts nonprofits are 13.5 times the national average.

These data were bolstered by a February 2015 article in *The Atlantic* magazine entitled "The Minneapolis Miracle" (although its content referred to both of the Twin Cities): "Minneapolis–St. Paul," wrote Derek Thompson, "is the headquarters for 19 Fortune 500 companies—more than any other metro its size—spanning retail (Target), health care (UnitedHealth), and food (General Mills)." The article went on to point out how the cities' housing and tax policies have produced solid, affordable neighborhoods with good schools.

The existence of these corporations, and their philanthropic arms, and of those good neighborhoods and schools, has a clear impact on the theater community here. The societal and cultural, and perhaps even the meteorological, climate of the Twin Cities has made the arts a key factor in the life of Minneapolis, St. Paul, and environs, providing a distinctive flavor to civic life. Many Twin Citians are regular theater patrons and enthusiasts, buying tickets, donating, and volunteering. Many have found their theater experiences to be moving, thrilling, and full of insight and laughter. So, too, have the practitioners.

Like most theater folk, I have a stock of moments from the ephemeral artwork of the live theater that stick with me. In my case, I hold a gesture from a particular actor talking about his roses, a downpour of rain on a Shakespearean army, an understudy going on to triumph and another one who couldn't remember his opening lines. As stage manager, I assigned four tap-dancing bellboys to accompany him through the musical, showing him where to go and reminding him what scene was coming up. One of them carried a script in a back pocket. From both backstage and the house, I carry memories of many rapt audiences catching their collective breath, laughing uncontrollably, being struck silent, and tearing up.

The conversations I've had in preparing this book have been full of those moments, intimate and revealing and powerful. I've drawn largely on the experiences of actors, designers, directors and artistic directors, and playwrights, as well as my own experiences as stage manager, production manager, and producing director. Other theater workers are less represented, although no less interesting and creative. I have the highest respect for music directors, choreographers, dramaturges, technicians—and the list goes on—but there simply wasn't room. Similarly, the wonderfully complex intersection of theater and music is not a focus here.

A few caveats. I have chosen to concentrate on the professional theater, and largely on the nonprofits, although there is a deep network of community and educational theater and fine commercial work here as well. Devised work, improvisational work, and comedy work are all less treated here, although no less admired. Another choice was to sidestep the traditional separation and rivalry between the cities of Minneapolis and St.

Paul; this is a book about *Twin Cities* theater, and I refer to it as such. Since each theater and show and performance is completely unique—one of the pleasures of the theater—few pronouncements can apply to all.

I hope this book will serve as a kind of introduction to the complicated and wonderful world of Twin Cities theater, and that the reader will enjoy the variety of voices and opinions found here. I've also included an annotated list of fifty-five Twin Cities theaters, which I offer as an invitation to browse. It's a community well worth browsing.

After all the years of running shows, I quite like it when the houselights go down to signal the start of a play and I've had nothing to do with it. Here, the equivalent gesture is turning the page. I invite you to turn it, and enjoy the show.

CHAPTER ONE

Process: The Very Beginning

Making theater is like working in a factory in which hundreds of opinionated people are assembling a complicated piece of machinery that has never been built before and will never be built again. All of them are working at top speed and most of them are working in the dark. Every once in a while, a brief flash of illumination will allow them to see each other or the work at hand; some don't glance up. Some workers are brilliant artisans; some are not. Some are justifiably egotistical, and some are needlessly so. The smallest decision that each one of these people makes in the course of his or her day could have a major impact on what everyone else is doing.

This factory contains a set of medieval craft shops, sprinkled with twentieth century techniques and materials, plus some cutting-edge technologies from the twenty-first. Some portions of the factory are antique, and some have never been tested before. Usually, a portion of the materials absolutely necessary for completion is missing. The factory is arranged in a pyramid, so that most of the people at the top can see portions of the work floor, but no one can see it all. It is overseen by a countdown clock as big as the sky, a clock that is always speeding up. Working in the factory, you are preparing for an approaching mass of random strangers who will look at the product and judge it. You can just hear their constant, barely audible tread. From that judgment the rest of your work life will flow, including the possibility that you will never work again.

Performing in the theater is like being a component in the engine driving that complicated machinery, knowing that you are necessary to make each performance march and sparkle. You bring nothing more to the task than your brain and will and body. You are surrounded by other pieces of the mechanism, but your hands are empty.

The theater and its product, the play, start simply with an idea and a single maker—in this case the playwright. Over time, the work becomes very complex and precarious, formed by many hands. But the idea isn't complete until it has materialized as an entire world populated with a jostling crowd of actors and artisans and designers and directors and presenters and producers and, most importantly, the audience—that mass of strangers—walking in to make their judgment.

Then, finally, you can see the entire product.

Let's posit the opening night of a new play. Let's assume, for the sake of the narrative, that the whole complex process has gone smoothly. Very smoothly. From the first flicker of the idea, event follows event in an orderly progression, without undue delays.

This never happens.

Five (or So) Years Before Opening Night:
Writing the Play

✓ *Writing the Play*	*Finding the Audience*
The Decision to Produce	*Rehearsing*
Assembling the Team	*Technical and Dress Rehearsals*
Casting the Show	*Opening Night*

Like other creative endeavors, the theater is a curious amalgam of relatively leisurely imaginative work crowned by an absolute deadline. The original work may set its own timetable, the necessary addition of collaborators might be random or deliberate, the envisioning of specifics extended or compressed. Once the date for opening night is set, however, there comes a drumbeat which cannot be ignored by any in the troupe, including and perhaps especially the playwright, the generator.

The indispensable writer E. B. White thought of the essayist as a self-liberated man, free to write about anything he damned well chose. "The essayist," White said in his foreword to the *Essays of E.B. White*, "arises in the morning and, if he has work to do, selects his garb from an unusually extensive wardrobe: he can pull on any sort of shirt, be any sort of person, according to his mood or his subject matter—philosopher, scold, jester, raconteur, confidant, pundit, devil's advocate, enthusiast."

The same may be said of playwrights. While there are rules to playwriting—and it's good to know them, even if you intend to break them—the rules are like a toolbox that can be applied to any kind of construction. The freedom of the playwright is the freedom to regard the world and choose any aspect of it as a subject for his or her art.

To be in the theater, you have to have a thick skin and an open heart. Except to be successful as a writer, you have to be really porous.

—PLAYWRIGHT KIRA OBOLENSKY

The work of the playwright is to create a slice of world, put it under a magnifying glass the size of a stage, and focus the audience to consider it. It is a complex and careful process, full of both craft and craftiness; during its few hours of performance, the play before the audience must be full of veracity. The audience members must suspend disbelief while the playwright holds their attention, and this demands that each note of the play ring true, or at least true to the playwright's intentions. Audiences sometimes see only what is before them—actors, scenery, music—forgetting where it all came from. It is good to give the playwright his or her due.

Like any writing work, playwriting is personal and arduous; it has no certain outcome. A playwright can take years to write a script—drafting and revising, thinking about plot and dialogue and motivation, working to keep the original idea alive. If the writer works solo, the idea will be subject to all the shifts and eddies of the work process, with only the writer's own voice to fuel its growth, shape it, and finish it.

In any case, the little flame of an idea can be delicate. Playwright Aditi Kapil believes that the most successful playwrights must be able to keep a play's original impulse alive: "The only person who knows what a play

Playwright, actor, and director Aditi Kapil.
(Photo by Bonni Allen)

ultimately can and should be is the play-wright. There are a lot of voices present in the development of a play, and that's great, but it's only great if you can hang on to your center."

Some of those voices provide invaluable input into the writing process through work-shops and readings. Barbara Field, a found-ing member of Minneapolis's Playwrights' Center, recalls happily that, in developing one play at the center, she was provided with twenty-two hours of rehearsal and reading time. "The play is not about just you and your computer; it's about actors interpreting your work. Theater is an intri-cate cooperative, and you need the actors to show you what's happening, to sit and read it, talk about it, give you suggestions about what was difficult for them. Twenty-two hours is a fortune!"

Kapil has read plays at the Playwrights' Center as an actor and also has workshopped a number of her scripts there as a playwright. She notes that the center's efforts in this regard have produced a pool of actors who excel at that kind of work. Kapil stresses the value of actors "being in the room with a playwright and being really flexible and really brave and open, just rushing at it head on. Having time in the rehearsal room with actors is a very big deal."

The laptop, the banged-up Remington, the quill and parchment are simply the mechanisms that carry the ideas of the playwright from his or her brain to the world. The original choice, the immense choice of what

Working a new version of *The Incredible Season of Ronnie Rabinovitz* at the History Theatre, with artistic director Ron Peluso *(standing center)*, playwright Eric Simonson *(far right)*, and company. (Photo by Jennifer E. Newell)

story and what characters to write about is the generative act of the theater. The play, once written, provides the platform on which all theater people crowd, bringing their bags of creativity and ambition, standing there to cast their own creative energies toward the cause of bringing the play to life.

If it ever does come to life, that is. Sometimes no one climbs aboard. Writing a play might mean years of unpaid work, with no guarantees that it will ever reach the stage. Playwrights say that they spend, or must spend, or sometimes, shaking their heads, *should* spend as much time working to see their plays produced as they do writing them in the first place. Sending out the play repeatedly, trying to ensure that it is read, and by the right person; talking about it and talking it up; researching producing organizations to find probable matches; working on his or her authorial brand; networking, which can also be called selling—these are parts of the process that do not always come naturally to a writer. They are, however, necessary. A play in the drawer has its satisfactions, but it is not finished until it is presented.

To young playwrights: Apply for things; get your work out there. You don't know who's going to read it, who's going to be on a panel. Maybe you'll win and then you'll get time to write the next thing.

—PLAYWRIGHT KIRA OBOLENSKY

A necessary balance between the art and the practical is often in the back of the writer's mind as she works. Regardless of its quality, will the play be *realized*? Will anyone ever produce it? Can they?

Even the largest and most successful producing organizations do few truly large-scale productions, and most are mightily inclined toward titles that just plain don't cost as much. Writing a fine play that requires eighteen actors, four sets including a functional ocean, and an orchestra of eight will limit your options; most producing organizations cannot and will not take a chance on a show so expensive and complex to mount. An oft-discussed Holy Grail, much simpler to produce, is a well-written and mountable one-set, three-character show. Writers who can produce those are both lauded and rewarded, since a substantial amount of playwright income is in royalties. Writing a play that is produced often and that sells well in good-sized houses is an entirely honorable career goal.

A sweet spot lies somewhere in this necessary balance between the art and the practical, and titles that hit that spot are one explanation for why traveling theatergoers sometimes see the same plays offered as they go from city to city, in both regional and commercial theaters. Another factor is name recognition. From a practical and marketing standpoint, producers like a title that people have already heard of. It makes filling the seats—another worthy goal—much easier.

Three (or So) Years Before Opening Night:
The Decision to Produce

✓ *Writing the Play*	*Finding the Audience*
✓ *The Decision to Produce*	*Rehearsing*
Assembling the Team	*Technical and Dress Rehearsals*
Casting the Show	*Opening Night*

The most direct intersection between art and practicality may take place in that moment when a producer decides to put a particular play on the stage. Each must ask one basic question: "Do I want to put on this play?"

- Is this play rich? Is it important? Do I love the story? Do I want to direct it? Or act in it? Is it something my heart longs to do? Will it feed my soul?
- Will it be good for my theater or my career? Will it round out my body of work? Take my organization in a new direction? Show my own work in a new light? Create or cement a relationship with a playwright to our mutual future benefit?
- Does it fit our mission? Does it fit with the other plays we are mounting that season?
- Will our audience love, be stimulated by, or be curious about this work? Will it be good for our audience?

The art of an artistic director is producing.

—ARTISTIC DIRECTOR JACK REULER

For some, any, or all of these reasons, all of them legitimate, *Chosen Play* is selected.

Most theater people are driven by creative aspiration, so the original impulse is probably an artistic one. Then, quite promptly, the impulse is assailed from all sides by the press of practical considerations. Now, the question is, "*Can* I put on this play?"

- Do I have the right actors for the key roles? Will those performers be available at the probable production time?
- Do I have the right director in mind? Is she or he available at that time?
- Do I have the right amount of time in our complex schedule for rehearsals and for building the show? (*Chosen Play* will take at least a month of rehearsal and six weeks of construction in the shops.)
- Do I have the right performing space for *Chosen Play*? Is our stage footprint large enough to accommodate the cast and the action of the play?
- Will my stakeholders be on board? What do other artistic staff members think about *Chosen Play*? How might the board of directors react? What are other area theaters planning for the same time?

And last, but never least, the producer considers, "Do I have the resources to put on the play?"

- Can we afford to pay the full company of actors, through *X* weeks of rehearsal and *Y* weeks of the run? What about the stage manager and the run crews (who will operate the lights and the sound and shift the scenery)? What about the fees for the director? The costume designer? The lighting designer? The sound designer? The choreographers and musicians? If any of these people must come from out of town, what are the additional travel and housing costs?
- Do our marketing people believe that the play will sell, at least enough to not sink our theater? Will we sell enough tickets to break even? Have we done a similar play in recent years and, if yes, how did it do? Can we do a longer run and, if we do, will the ticket income outstrip the additional costs?

- What about the physical creation of *Chosen Play*? Is it a big costume show? Is it in period? Will costumes have to be rented or built, or can they be designed from local thrift store purchases? Are any of the necessary costumes already in our stock? What about scenery and props? Is it a big show, requiring lots of built scenery and weeks of time with the scene shop and its artisans?
- Are the rights available? Are there royalties? Script costs? What will it cost to sell those very important tickets—advertising, promotion, graphic design?

Considerable mathematics is involved. In the final analysis, does *Chosen Play* survive this implacable gauntlet of constrictions? Concessions are inevitable. Can the original artistic impulse still be discerned through the compromises?

Choosing a title as part of a season—artistically rewarding, pleasingly balanced, and logistically and financially possible—may be the most critical skill of a theater's artistic leadership.

According to Children's Theatre Company (CTC) artistic director Peter Brosius, CTC starts with a commitment to new work: "There is no existing canon of extraordinary work for theater for young people, so we see it as our responsibility, as the leader in our field, to build it and to make it." At any given moment, he says, the theater has up to twelve projects in the making, some of which are wholly original and some of which are adaptations. "We work toward which of these projects together can make a season that can cover a panoply of concerns, from new work to reimagined classics to work that speaks to the diverse communities of our nation. And to the various ages that we serve, as well as keep the doors open."

"In addition," Brosius says, "we scour the planet. I'm busy looking at theaters and festivals from across the globe; there's a series of presenters, producers, festivals that I scout regularly. Then I start talking to my colleagues, and these colleagues are global. There is extraordinary work happening in this field, whether it's in London or in Rotterdam or in Johannesburg; there is work all over that we want to explore." Brosius distinguishes between "presenters," who do not always produce their own work, and "producers," who create projects from the ground up.

"One of the great things about this art form," continues Brosius, "is its elasticity and the fact that it can speak in so many aesthetic languages. So we put together a dream season. And then we budget it. And then things change." The Children's Theatre Company, he says, prepared at least twenty budget scenarios as they settled on their fiftieth anniversary season in 2015–16.

Mu Performing Arts artistic director Randy Reyes holds the audience in his mind throughout the process, with a long list of specific considerations: "What do you want the audience experience of your theater company to be? Who is this audience and what do they need? What stories haven't we told yet? What stories, what communities, haven't been represented?" Reyes wants to challenge the audience and not just give them something they like. He also considers ways to increase the size of his audience.

Growing and nurturing the audience was a key question for Reyes while he ran an outdoor theater company called the Strange Capers. It lasted for four summers, until, he says, "our day jobs got too busy." The theater's mission was to put on classical plays, giving young artists opportunities to act in free performances outside. To reach an audience, Reyes notes, "You have to make it very accessible, make Shakespeare fun. Make it clear, and excite people. And have a diverse-looking cast. You have to reflect the audience that you want to attract."

In considering titles, Reyes adds, "There are always 'dream plays' that you want to do. You always have to be listening for what's happening now and for exciting things coming up in the culture. . . . What's great about this community is that we can take risks, and people will support it. If we couldn't take risks, we would be a for-profit theater and we'd just do Disney plays or Disney movies that get turned into plays for the masses. But we can take risks and that's why it's so important that not-for-profits exist. Because we cannot be reliant on selling tickets for our stories to be told."

Sarah Bellamy, co–artistic director of Penumbra Theatre, speaks about the challenges of having to pick and choose which plays to do: "One of the things I think all artistic directors and producers struggle with is, 'why

Randy Reyes as playwright David Henry Hwang in *Yellow Face*, presented by Mu Performing Arts at the Guthrie Theater. Directed by Rick Shiomi. (Photo by Michal Daniel)

don't we have more money so that we can do all of them?' We've only got a limited amount of real estate, and how are we going to use it?"

Filters apply. Penumbra is committed to producing work from the classical black theater canon and also to showcasing new voices to provide "an opportunity to look back and to look forward," says Bellamy. "We look for plays that are really unafraid and bold in their engagement of social justice issues. We look for scripts that are exciting, and of course we always think about size. It's very difficult to produce a play with fifteen, sixteen, twenty people in it; in fact, sometimes those plays don't even get read. And we look for plays that are creatively exciting to do."

Sarah Bellamy, co-artistic director of Penumbra Theatre.
(Photo by Ann Marsden)

Bellamy stresses that, as an African American arts organization, Penumbra wants to represent the full breadth and depth and vitality of the African American experience, but, she points out, there are only a certain number of slots to do that each season. "We try to be really well balanced."

The decision for Michael Robins and Bonnie Morris, executive producing director and producing director, respectively, of Illusion Theater, is made more complex by the fact that much of the work they present is brand new. They have a long history of working supportively with playwrights, providing them with both commission and freedom. Robins says, "To me, it's the people. You want to commit to the artist."

Playwright Jeffrey Hatcher is appreciative. "Most theaters," he says, "commission a play, doing so with a particular subject in mind: an adaptation, a social issue, a collaboration, etc. In my experience, Illusion is also willing, far more than most other theaters, to commission the playwright. They will ask a playwright 'what is it that you have been itching to write, dying to write?' Then they're willing to pay for it. That is increasingly rare in the American theater."

Morris adds that, when they first started out, Illusion generated all its own work. "We still have that tremendous faith in the creative process. Deciding to do something that hasn't been finished yet puts tremendous pressure on our people. How do you describe it? Can children come? How long is it? And changing it all the time puts a lot of pressure on my design team. They're going to cut props and costumes, they're going to cut set."

"What happens here, though," says Morris, "is people get a fragrance

Michael Robins, founder and executive producing director of Illusion Theater. (Photo by Lauren Falk)

of what's coming into being and get really exhilarated by it. Something's cooking here.... We look at what's happening in our times, and then we look at what we could produce that would have something to do with what's going on."

The choosing is not easy. History Theatre artistic director Ron Peluso, whose theater commissions playwrights to write "the real stories of real people" from the region, notes that, in many ways, "I have the challenge and burden of deciding whose history gets told, what lives to honor, what issues of social justice, labor, or family to tell."

The artistic impulse. The mission. The practical considerations. The desired effect on the audience. Choosing the title is a complex business, and when the show to be produced will tour, a host of other issues come into play. Back in 1980, Christine Tschida was the outreach director at the Guthrie and Liviu Ciulei was the incoming artistic director. Tschida says she cringes when she thinks back to the ultimatum with which she greeted him before the ink had dried on his contract. She recalls her speech to Ciulei this way:

> Mr. Ciulei, even though it's barely 1980, we need to know what production we'll tour in 1982. The title has to be well known, familiar, but not over-exposed, nor the kind of show done by community theaters or the local high school. It has to be sophisticated and interesting enough to attract audiences in several big cities, but inoffensive to the more conservative communities we might visit in the Bible Belt. The show must also appeal to teachers and

students, so that we can play student matinees. If the title is too
new we won't be able to get the touring rights. . . . But be careful
if you choose a classic, because they are generally large-cast shows.
The touring production can't have more than ten characters, and
the characters should be no older than fifty because it is so hard
to get mature actors to tour. The setting, of course, has to be a unit
one-location set, and that set has to fit within a forty-foot trailer
because it would be impossible to freight more than that amount
around the country.

The title that ran this gauntlet in 1982, and represented the work of a
brand-new Guthrie artistic director to a region, was *The Rainmaker*.

Every theater in town, in every season, chooses titles, finding the necessary balance between the artistic impulse and the practical. The artistic conversations and aspirations are ongoing, and so are the necessary
restrictions. Some version of these conversations is taking place right now,
at this very moment, in backstage offices large and small, all over town.

CHAPTER TWO

The Nature of Theater Work

for any thing so overdone is
from the purpose of playing, whose end, both at the
first and now, was and is, to hold, as 'twere, the
mirror up to nature; to show virtue her own feature,
scorn her own image, and the very age and body of
the time his form and pressure.

—William Shakespeare, *Hamlet*

Live performance in physical proximity to an audience has an immediacy that is absent from other visual storytelling forms, such as television or film. Dramatic performance might be most similar to the act of reading a book, in which the words travel, undiluted, from the author to the imagination of the reader. Except that drama happens through the medium of the theater, which means it happens through, and in, a crowd.

The individuals in an audience enter the theater in a wide variety of states of mind. Something went right today; something went wrong. The dishwasher broke down. You noticed a spot of rust on your car in the lot. You are beginning to wonder about your job, your girlfriend, your life. The ticket was expensive, the title obscure. You can't pronounce the name of the playwright; how are you going to talk about it with your companions? The other playgoers look better dressed and smarter than you. The lobby is crowded, the house full. Every person in the audience is thinking something like these things; they are all carrying some kind of dishwasher.

And yet, there comes a hush. When the houselights go down, every person in the audience stops, dropping their dishwashers and their boyfriends and their jobs and their lives. They settle their coats and purses and put their programs in their laps. With a collective breath, they turn their eyes to the stage, where a mystery is rising before them. It is the setting for a different life, imaginary yet palpably real. It is complex, populated with incident and character. They give it their complete attention. On stage, people step from the dark into the light and begin to speak. The people in the seats listen. On a good night, the connection is complete and instantaneous. On a really good night, the connection lasts all the way through to the final bows.

This condition, a condition of communication, is evident in the faces of the people in the theater. As the lights go down, something else comes up. It is the moment when the artifice of the play joins with the real life of the house; or when the real lives of the actors join with the fictional life of the play; or when the live idea of the playwright joins with the live ideas in the audience's minds.

In the theater, everyone in the circle of the stage participates in the event. It is the condensing of all that juice—the collective energy from both the tellers and the watchers—that makes the theater luminous. This living web of audience and performer, playwright and story, fosters ideas and fires the emotions—avarice or despair, high humor or low, love or spiritual yearning. It is the voltage that springs the play and its ideas from the page and brings them to the stage in front of the audience.

In 1964, one year after opening his eponymous theater in Minneapolis, Tyrone Guthrie spoke of the nature of the theater, and its enduring power, in his book *A New Theatre:* "I believe that a theatre where live actors perform to an audience which is there in the flesh before them, will survive all threats from powerfully organized industries which pump prefabricated dramas out of cans and blowers and contraptions of one kind or another. . . . It will survive as long as mankind demands to be amused, terrified, instructed, shocked, corrupted and delighted by tales told in a manner that will always remain mankind's most vivid and powerful manner of telling a story, I believe."

In the decades since those words were written, there has been an astonishing proliferation of "cans and blowers and contraptions of one kind or another." The theater survives.

A primary pleasure for all those who work in the theater is the practice of lifting words from a page and using them as the basis for creating a complete and dynamic world. Theater work is constantly reinvented, since each production has the freedom and the mandate to remake the original with its own aesthetics and in its own time. Think of the many versions of, for example, *Romeo and Juliet*. There is the traditional doublets-and-hose look, but there are also renditions set in every possible period and locale, and a musical or two, including one based in New York City where the key sword fight became a knife fight (*West Side Story*). Many film iterations, ballets, symphonic treatments, operas. The power of the story, with its young lovers and its harsh conflicts, provides a template for each group of artists that attempts it.

For its enthusiasts, whether they are workers or aficionados, the theater offers an array of intellectual rewards and a dizzying landscape of possibilities. Like most work in the arts, the forms of drama are as complex, malleable, and quirky as the human minds that execute them, or have ever executed them. Speaking only of the western canon, classical theaters regularly present work more than two thousand years old—from ancient Greece—and even more regularly work from the Elizabethan period—all that Shakespeare. A level of familiarity with the dramatic literature of the past is one of the lasting pleasures of the theater. That these stories are still heard and brought to the stage is testament to their enduring power. Good plays, the plays that have lasted, provide a direct and living window into the times and minds of the playwrights and the original settings. But in addition to recording what was important to people at the time they were written, the storylines that endure also reflect what is important now and will likely be important into an undetermined future. In television's *Star Trek*, the stalwart captain reads *Moby-Dick* while hurtling through the galaxies on a starship. It is likely that, a few decks down, the drama group aboard the *Enterprise*, and there certainly is one, is working on a staged reading of *A Midsummer Night's Dream*, laughing at the misadventures of the lovers.

Even when a script is reinterpreted, audience members are treated to a rich glimpse into the past. Rich, because the theater is a human art form. Each theater person, from the playwright to the extra, brings his or her sense of contemporary humanity to the work. All that collective humanity, on stage in front of your eyes and your brain, makes a very rich stew. What we call the classics survive through time for a reason.

"Our responsibility as artists," says Jungle Theater artistic director and actor Bain Boehlke, "is to seek and tell the truth of the human experience, which is the one we live. That's what the great plays talk about—Euripides, Sophocles, Shakespeare. They let us know that people were always the same. They have not changed. It's the human heart, it's about what takes us off the target of cultural and societal harmony. How do we live together? That's the big question, still the creative question."

It's easy to forget that the "classics" were all once new works that sprang from a particular culture and period. The same is true in our time. New work written for the stage can, quite literally, be about anything, and the Twin Cities audience regularly has the opportunity to see world-premiere performances in many different venues and in many different styles. Sometimes these new works cross over into commercial success (*Triple Espresso* and *Church Basement Ladies* come to mind), and sometimes they find a different path.

At Workhaus Collective, playwrights also function as artistic directors. Another fine spot to taste the huge variety of brand-new writing is the nationally renowned Playwrights' Center. Here are excerpts from descriptions of new plays read or workshopped at the Playwrights' Center during the 2014–15 season:

- "A tragi-comedy about shifting gender politics and the ways we learn to adapt" (*Forget Me Not When Far Away*, by Kira Obolensky)
- "Sixteen-year-old Thuy dreams of joining her GI father's American family" (*Dust*, by Qui Nguyen)

- "Bringing fierce guitar playing and swing to gospel music, Sister Rosetta Tharpe was a legend in her time" (*Marie and Rosetta*, by George Brant)
- "A meditation on authenticity and class collision" (*The REALNESS: the second break beat play*, by Idris Goodwin)
- "This is Florida, with some of the toughest drug laws in the nation" (*Romeo and Naomi Ramirez*, by Kathryn Walat)
- ". . . the effects of gun violence on their city" (*Cocked*, by Sarah Gubbins)
- "An American tragedy about the wages of fear" (*The Absence of Weather*, by Ken Urban)
- "What it really means to be committed, what it means to be married, and what it means to be queer" (*Le Switch*, by Philip Dawkins)

The thinking and topics of these playwrights is utterly contemporary, and their variety illustrates that theatrical endeavor is a thoughtful line of work, requiring and rewarding close observation of human behavior. Plays presented in workshop mode invite additional study and the exciting possibility of seeing them again and later, in a more developed form. The playwrights, of course, devoutly wish for the same.

The fascinations of the theater are many, and of sufficient breadth to attract and sustain the interest of a wide variety of people. Its nature is multifaceted.

Rehearsing and performing a play can be a kind of deep-study experience. As Guthrie Theater stage manager Chris Code notes, "One of the really cool things about this job is that every new show is like going back to school, in the best possible way. Along with everybody in the cast and company, we get a wonderful education on a whole new world, for every play we do. We get to spend a quality amount of time, and a quantity amount of time, sitting around a table discussing the texts, tearing it apart, figuring out exactly what these people mean. The context, the milieu, the place these characters are in the world, the history of the time period. For a new play, we sometimes have the playwright right there. We have a dramaturge

Stage manager Chris Code in his program shot from the Guthrie Theater. (Photo by Mike Habermann)

who can tell you about any aspect of the world of the play, where it fits in history and society. It's a remarkable experience."

Playwright Barbara Field, when she became a dramaturge at the Guthrie, was offered a choice by then–artistic director Michael Langham and had no doubt what she wanted to concentrate on. "When I was hired, he said, 'Do you want to work on new plays at the Second Stage or classics on the main stage?' I didn't hesitate a microsecond.

Playwright Barbara Field. (Photo by Mike Habermann)

Actors *(left to right)* Barbra Berlovitz, Sarah Agnew, and Cynthia Lohman in *Tartuffe* at Theatre de la Jeune Lune, 1999. Lighting by Marcus Dilliard, costumes by Sonya Berlovitz. (Photo by Michal Daniel)

I wanted to know how Shakespeare got a person in through a door. Or out the door. My immersion in the classics just sharpened my sense of theater. You can't become intimate with *Tartuffe* without seeing how Molière did it." She adds that she is a "glutton for craft," and that came from her time at the Guthrie.

Lighting designer Marcus Dilliard came to the theater after dabbling in studies as a biologist and an electrical engineer, but by the time he settled on the theater, he had let go of everything else. He says of his decision, "It was the fact that it [theater] was constantly mysterious. It felt like something you could dig into for a long, long time and not understand, and not get bored with. There was a long way to go with it."

Artistic director Peter Rothstein of Theater Latté Da broadened and deepened his theatrical thinking as a result of an invitation to direct, received when he was still trying to make a living as an actor. At the time, he says, "Auditioning was what I wanted; I had no vision beyond the 550 section [the audition section of the newspaper's classified ads]. I hadn't been thinking any more broadly than that. What impact did I want to have on the world, what issues were important to me?" A colleague offered him a directorial slot and asked if there was a writer he wanted to work with or a topic he was interested in exploring. "I really didn't have an answer, and that was a wake-up. It was important to me that I have a vision beyond the 550 section."

Peter Rothstein, artistic director and founder of Theater Latté Da, offstage at the Pantages Theatre. (Photo by Regina Marie Williams)

A signature element of the theater is that it is far from a solitary activity—even one-person shows have writers and directors and designers and crew—and the act of making something with others is another pleasure, or at least a condition, of the work. Everyone comes into the room together, bringing their talents and their ideas; everyone has choices to make. The end product is the result of all those decisions together, and it is experienced together.

As Illusion Theater's Bonnie Morris explains, people in the theater understand that they are supposed to create and that one of its pleasures is to create with other people. "In the work world," she says, "not everybody gets to be in a team, or in a collaborative group, where you're all working towards the same aim. We all believe that together we're going to make something that's bigger than anything that any one of us could create."

Costume designer Sonya Berlovitz began her career with the influential Theatre de la Jeune Lune, where, she says, creative collaboration was everything. "The theater thought of all the elements involved—design, music, actor, directors—that we are all on an even plane and that we all brought something to the work. In that way every part of the work feels valuable, and you're making a contribution, and getting to be as creative as possible. There's a lot of freedom in that. Sometimes something comes out that you would never have imagined, that might be even more interesting."

It is a kind of secular communion, based on communication and collaboration, both among the workers and with the watchers.

Playwright Barbara Field recalls standing backstage and listening to an actor do a speech from one of her works: "I had a sort of thrill of being naked in front of everyone if they could but read the messages. I had exposed myself in a way that I'd never thought I could do. That was thrilling; it's a thrill to hear scenes work. You get excited by it."

Playwright Aditi Kapil had a similar experience; she thinks that connectivity is part of the nature of the theater, and that collaboration among the artists is elemental to the process. In her "Forum Theatre" interview with Jacqueline Lawton, she said, "I saw my story get communicated with so many layers of intricacy and individuality that I couldn't possibly have created on my own. I watched the audience as closely as I watched the play. Seeing them love my messy, confused characters made that thing that fills your world, made me feel less lonely in the world, feel like other people thought about these things, too."

Ten Thousand Things Theater performs without a stage or stage lights, in a rectangle of chairs; performance runs begin in homeless shelters, prisons, low-income housing, and community centers and finish with ticketed public events. Artistic director Michelle Hensley often welcomes the audience and reminds them of the obvious: the actors can see them, and they can see each other. There is no sheltering darkness. The houselights do not go down; the sight of each other can be profound and revealing. "For me," says Hensley, "the pleasure of theater is the joy of connecting with someone who has never seen theater before, someone who has actually entered the room thinking he or she will not like what's going on. Finding out that I have something in common with someone who I thought was incredibly different than me—that makes it worth all the incredible and sometimes excruciating things we have to go through to get to that moment."

Playwright Kira Obolensky works closely with Ten Thousand Things, in part because she appreciates the connection to be made with unconventional audiences. She says, "There's an extraordinary pleasure in writing plays and having them be seen by people who are hungry for stories. One of the pitfalls we fall into in our form is that people who often go to the

Michelle Hensley, artistic director of Ten Thousand Things, introduces their production of *Man of La Mancha* at Hennepin County's women's correction facility. (Photo courtesy of Ten Thousand Things)

theater—well, they are people who often go to the theater. They've seen so many stories, they're sort of filled up with stories. Suddenly it becomes less about that sheer thrill of a story connecting with a human life."

Bonnie Morris of Illusion Theater expands the idea of connection, believing that theater is important to the soul, for both the workers and the audience. In her 2014 acceptance speech for the Lifetime Achievement Award at the Ivey Awards, which celebrate Twin Cities professional theater, she said, "What we who work in the theater get to do is what I believe we all were meant to do: to create, to generate, to invite, to hear poetry. To be part of music-making. We imagine ourselves outside of our names, our jobs, our zip codes. We hear stories, tell stories, and let the stories themselves lead us to a deeper knowing of who we are and why we are here." Another credo, this one from writer Alice Walker, is on the wall of

Morris's office at the Illusion: "If art doesn't make us better, then what on earth is it for?"

"To be in a creative space," says Morris, "to have people writing words, speaking poetry, making music, [to] have people risk in front of you, be vulnerable, with a faith that we're going to create something that matters to other people, why would you not want to do this? How could you not choose to do this?"

Playwright Aditi Kapil has a clear idea of what theater is for and reflects that belief in every work she writes: "What the arts in a healthy society do is put us in dialogue with each other about things that are deep. The things we talk about are things that lay in the area of the soul and the subconscious and feelings and human connectivity."

"The reason I write a play is to put us in dialogue about our common humanity," says Kapil. "The reason I do it for theater specifically is because there's something uniquely powerful about gathering in a room as a bunch of people. To me, the moment of theater simmers in the air between the performance and the audience. We all feel and understand and experience something together. Hopefully it shifts your world just a little bit. Hopefully you bring that home with you and it trickles out into your own life and keeps going."

"It's on me," she continues, "to start the conversations I think are necessary right now, and to push forward the conversations that I think we need to have right now. There's no one else who's thinking about the things I'm obsessed about. It's my job to go ahead and obsess about them, and not allow myself to be swayed from the things that I think are really important. It's my responsibility."

Kapil takes her own work, and the work of the theater, very seriously. "It's deep, what we do," she says. "If we could explain it in a few words, we wouldn't need to do it. If I start writing a new play, it's going to take me three freaking years, and I'm probably never going to get paid for those three years of my life. So it had better be important enough to me to be putting these thoughts out into the world. It's a really big deal when I embark on a new project, because it has to be important. It really, really does."

Actor Anna Sundberg's father is a pastor and, although she says she has

H. Adam Harris in *The Way of Water*, with Hope Cervantes, from Frank Theatre at the Playwrights' Center. Directed by Wendy Knox. (Photo by E. G. Bailey)

never felt very religious, she thinks they are in some ways in the same business. "I asked him once why he was called and I could have written down verbatim everything he said and it was why I do theater. A lot of us are here searching for the same thing. Why are we here? What does it mean to be a human being? How do we connect to other people? What does it mean to make mistakes and fail and struggle?"

"Why do we keep doing this?" she asks. "It's mostly to figure out what we're doing. Most of us just want to feel like we're not alone. When I watch a great play, I feel I'm not alone."

With some theater practitioners, the words *sacred* and *spiritual* and *important* occur again and again. When actor H. Adam Harris talks about the audience, he says, "The art is about the constant exchange of what I give to them and what they give to me. What they give me is the inspiration to continue to give, so we get in this beautiful sort of cycle. I always use 'inspire,' which is 'to take the breath in.' They give me life."

Actor Ricardo Vazquez learned from an influential teacher that the stage is a sacred place. He says, "In order for you to take a step on it, you have to be a hundred and ten percent committed in your every fiber, your every fluid ounce, everything of your being. If you don't do that, you don't belong there; you need to step aside. That's the kind of energy you need. To achieve that is the discipline and the gamble of every opportunity you have as an actor.

T. Mychael Rambo in *Caroline, or Change* at the Guthrie Theater. (Photo by Michal Daniel)

A gamble because there's absolutely no way to guarantee that you'll be able to do it."

"We all have a course and a journey in life, we all have a message that we live to speak to, and this happens to be mine," says actor T. Mychael Rambo. "It has saved my life; it has kept me whole; it has given me something to live by and to live through."

"Some people find great joy in numbers, or finding what happens with bacteria under a microscope, or preparing fabulous meals," says Rambo. "For me, it's being able to find the fabric and the story and the nuance behind a character, or unveiling some forgotten moment that an audience never thought of. Or to leave feeling that someone finally saw and understood what it meant to be my character. That's really important. It's something I love and I'm very driven, committed, and intended to do."

Designer Kate Sutton-Johnson expresses her connection quite simply; she feels most inspired during live performance. "If I'm spiritual or religious at all, it's in the theater. There. I almost always cry at a curtain call. There's something about when I have my heart in a show that I'm watching. Then I watch the actors sort of turn back into themselves. I find that really moving."

She is not the only one to be moved, either in the audience or in the stage house.

Jungle Theater artistic director Bain Boehlke, who produces and directs, designs and acts, put the premise plainly when he accepted the Ivey

Bain Boehlke in *The Gin Game* at the Jungle Theater. Set design by Bain Boehlke. (Photo by Michal Daniel)

Lifetime Achievement Award in 2011. He expressed the nature of theater in this way: "I like to be fully alive, and theater is the most living, dancing connection to life that I have found."

The intellectual, artistic, and spiritual rewards of theater can be harnessed for a discernible and distinct purpose: social change. Jack Reuler, the founder and artistic director of Mixed Blood Theatre, says the point is not how good the show

Bonnie Morris, producing artistic director at Illusion Theater, with the company of the Keepin' It Real program, in which high school actors perform for younger girls. (Photo courtesy of Illusion Theater)

Jack Reuler, artistic director and founder of Mixed Blood Theatre. (Photo by Dale Connelly)

is, or how many people show up. Rather, "That is a great means to an end. But the end is actually: how do people's attitudes and behaviors and, ultimately, policies change as a result of what you've done? You need to be great at all those other things to get to that point."

For Reuler, the rewards of theater work "are the unbelievable array of people that one gets to meet in the life in the theater. The portals that this theater has opened for me to go out into the public and private sector, to be able to deal with health care, to be able to deal with the legal profession, to deal with corporate America, and to use theater to actually change the way people do things. The theater is a tool for social change, and you can actually see change happen."

There can, of course, be more than one good purpose. Each person or group of people who starts a theater or a project has the opportunity to shape this amorphous beast into what they envision, and to set it in motion with particular intention. It is entirely honorable (and historically justified) when the theater has the intention of making money. And entertainment can be a mission; an evening spent laughing brings something light and bright and necessary into the world. The theater is fun.

Director John Miller-Stephany tries to get a clear sense of the playwright's intention when he starts work on a project. "And sometimes," he told Minnesota Playlist's Paul de Cordova, "the playwright's intention might be as simple as to make 'em laugh. *The Importance of Being Earnest* is one of the greatest plays ever written, but it's really not about anything except some fantastic language and some really good laughs."

Actor T. Mychael Rambo believes that "comedy and shenanigans and satire" are just as important as serious drama. "Theater is a verb, not just a noun," he says. "It's 'to theater.' It's to live, to breathe, to have a range of emotional energy and arc. It's an action, and as an active space there's a lot of doing, and there are a lot of different ways to approach the doing. It's important that there be a range of how we access and enter into the space of theater. There are so many different individuals that inhabit the planet; there need to be just as many ways of finding ourselves in the space of theater."

No theater form is intrinsically more important than another. "I don't believe in one high church of theater," says actor and singer Bradley Greenwald, whose work spans both the serious and the comic. "To me, any discipline should be respected because, as a performer, you know how hard

Bradley Greenwald in *I Am My Own Wife* at the Jungle Theater. Greenwald played thirty characters in the one-man show. Direction and set design by Joel Sass. (Photo by Michal Daniel)

it is in the act of performance to pay attention to so much detail and hair-splitting execution. When you see someone executing the same care and respect for their discipline as you would in your own, then of course it needs to be respected. I would never say 'that's a lower kind of theater and this is a higher kind of theater.' It's all work."

All theater people, whether serious-minded or light, performers or not, understand that the bedrock of the theater is made up of work and skill. "Act well your part; there all the honour lies," said the eighteenth-century English poet Alexander Pope in his *Essays on Man*, and the adage is posted in thousands of high school theater departments all across the land. There's another adage, less posted, but no less true: Perform it badly and it's painful for everyone. That's why it's called theater *work*.

Here's what I enjoy about being in shows: sometimes what we do is a craft, sometimes what we do is a job, and sometimes it feels like art.

—ACTOR KURT KWAN (MINNESOTA PLAYLIST PROFILE
    BY PAUL DE CORDOVA)

For those who find their work in it, the theater can be a great source of happiness, of companionship, and of vitality. It is also, nearly always, a very tough row to hoe. Its joys—unbridled creativity, intense work pace, fellowship—are also part of its conditions—its difficulty, uncertainty, and occasional brutality. Both the joys and the difficulties are part of the nature of theater work. In *As You Like It*, Shakespeare wrote, "Sweet are the uses of adversity, / Which, like the toad, ugly and venomous, / Wears yet a precious jewel in his head." In the theater, there's a good deal of adversity to go around.

Set designer Kate Sutton-Johnson makes it plain: "I think it's a combination of how much does the work mean to you, and how much are you willing to tolerate, because it is really hard. If it doesn't really, really bring you joy and fulfill you, it is not worth it, because it is a really hard life."

As Park Square Theatre artistic director Richard Cook puts it, "The only reason you would become a manager or producer or an artistic director is because it sparks something deep in you that fulfills something essential in your life. Because it is still a sacrificial profession. It just is."

Wendy Knox, artistic director of Frank Theatre, has alternated work in her own theater with work for other institutions, as she wrote in Minnesota Playlist: "There have been times when I have wondered, 'Can I keep on doing this? Should I keep on doing this?' Like other kindred spirits who also move between work in larger organizations and their own shops, their individual work, we all wrestle with the joys, the pains, and the trade-offs in our circumstances. The thrill of having your own shop is balanced by the pain of having to do everything yourself on a shoestring budget; the opportunity of working in more well-heeled venues is undercut by the need to follow someone else's rules and priorities when you are a guest in their house."

The work schedule in the theater, for example, is specific and largely inflexible. Freelancers do not control their own schedules, and they must be entirely responsive to others' decisions about shows and production periods. If you are involved in performances, your work life takes place on evenings and weekends, opposite to the civilian workaday world. That work life is absorbing and can sometimes blot out the non-theater world, which somehow seems less vivid and immediate. Shows come and go, and seasons go by. Sometimes the world goes by without your notice.

The work is both episodic and cyclical. "The hard part for the freelancers," says Cook, "is the feast or famine problem. There are intense periods of production in the fall and again after the first of the year, when we're all calling talent and saying 'can you come over?' And then there will be fallow periods where there's nothing. It is really hard to become your own personal financial manager, to even that out in some way."

Pay scales differ drastically not just with the size of the theater but also with its policies and with its union affiliations. Actors' Equity Association, which represents actors and stage managers, has arrangements with roughly two dozen theaters in the Twin Cities at this writing. The arrangements vary from contracts that cover all conditions of employment to special letters of agreement. Directors and designers have their own unions. Once they become union members, theater workers may be able to depend on higher paychecks and benefit contributions. In most cases, however, they will no longer be free to take any job they wish.

Paychecks are famously small in the theater; the number of workweeks can also be very small. In 2014, then–Actors' Equity Association president Nick Wyman, a New York–based actor who once worked briefly at the Guthrie, wrote in his presidential column that he had worked only two weeks in the previous year. (One assumes he had a sufficiency of non-AEA work.) The difficult calculation of making a living, or even paying one's rent, necessarily includes both size of paychecks and number of workweeks. College and university training, or conservatory training, can increase skill and sometimes visibility, but can also mean substantial student debt.

Second or third jobs, part-time work, teaching, unemployment—all these are likely to be part of life in the theater. There are jobs that pay the bills and there are jobs that relate to the stage work. If you are an actor, those might include voice-overs, commercials, or television or film. There might be an available connection with a Twin Cities museum; some regularly employ theater professionals as playwrights, actors, designers, and technicians in their exhibition or educational programs.

To emerging actors: You have to understand what you're going to sacrifice. If theater is your primary interest, then making a living is your secondary interest.

—DIRECTOR RICK SHIOMI

Or there are the hyphens—the director-designers, the designer-technicians, and the like—and, for some lucky theater workers, the ability to find satisfaction in more than one arena. H. Adam Harris is one of those; he says, "I think of myself as an actor and a teacher. I don't think of myself as

H. Adam Harris directing *Awake* at Penumbra Theatre's Summer Institute, a leadership program for teens. (Photo used courtesy of Allen Weeks)

an actor who teaches because they need the money, and I don't think of myself as a teacher who just wants to act. It's very important to me that I continue to live a life that allows me to be both. This town has made room for me to do that, and I wouldn't give it up." Many Twin Cities theaters offer classes of various kinds—and need theater professionals to teach them.

The theater life may be easier for young theater professionals just entering the workforce; age makes a difference, and combining freelance work and nonprofit work can be a particular challenge. Jack Reuler of Mixed Blood Theatre notes, "When you get to an age where you want certain luxuries—like lunch—people leave nonprofit-dom. The number of sixty-year-old actors and the number of twenty-eight-year-old actors is quite different."

Director Joel Sass is familiar with the difficulties actors can face in putting together a work life. He says, "A career in the arts can be mercurial. A lot of it is dependent on building long-term artistic relationships and being able to identify and leverage short-term opportunities. Patience and fortitude are essential; some actors are not born to be ingénues and have to wait until they're thirty or more before exploding into success as dramatic or character actors."

In the meantime, their year's portfolio might have two roles, and a great deal of work unrelated to the theater. This kind of rhythm can go on for years.

A great deal of theater life depends on talent, and that, Sass says, is one thing people don't like to talk about. "We all feel vulnerable," he says. "Our talent could evaporate at any moment, or it could become antique or irrelevant. If we artists expect to enjoy a viable career for twenty or thirty years, we have to be committed to stretching our abilities; we can't risk becoming predictable. Instead, we have to exist in a state of constant self-discovery, renovation, and renewal of our talents in order to continue offering something new to the cultural dialogue."

It can sometimes be difficult for theater people to find a way to demonstrate their capabilities and talent. The best way to see an actor's range and

Joel Sass and company in technical rehearsal for *Pericles* at the Guthrie Lab. Lighting by Marcus Dilliard. (Photo by Michal Daniel)

skill is to see them performing. Although the audition process provides some pathway, an actor who is not performing is not being seen. Directors and designers cannot audition, and their portfolios and clips and show photos, however elaborate and full of praise, are hampered by the inevitable fact that they are static remnants of a living art form.

In any part of the theater, recognition and economic independence can be a long time coming. Artistic director Michelle Hensley remembers: "I think the first ten years of Ten Thousand Things I primarily made my income doing other freelance work. When I was, I think, thirty-five, I'd been in the Twin Cities maybe four or five years. I had to take a temp job in some kind of place that manufactured ball bearings for automobiles; I was working in the filing department. So here I am, thirty-five years old, graduated from an Ivy League college. I imagine I was the only one of my classmates that wasn't making six figures and for sure one of the few graduates still doing temp jobs. And I just put my head down on the desk in the filing room where no one else could see and I just cried."

Why did she keep going? "I'm not sure," says Hensley now, "except that I felt it was the only thing that I really wanted to do. And I've always been about trying to make my life have meaning by giving back in the way I can best do that." Her Ten Thousand Things theater is regularly celebrated as a lynchpin of Twin Cities theater, and a model for other theaters nationwide.

Well-known actor Sally Wingert remembers a period of six years, before she obtained her Actors' Equity Association union card, when she waited tables or tended bar in addition to acting. Since the age of twenty-four, she says, she has made her living in the theater, which she describes as "a complete miracle." She continues, "I hate not having job security and I wish I was paid more, but that's kind of all I wish for. If the primary goal of my life was to make more money," she says, "then I could figure out a way to do that. I'm happy doing what I'm doing. And I would put my joy at my job against almost anybody else and say 'try to match me for how much fun this is to do.'"

Still, Wingert says, "Even to this day, I scope out restaurants thinking that I might have to go back to waiting tables."

Sally Wingert as Peggy
Guggenheim in *Woman Before
a Glass* for the Minnesota
Jewish Theatre Company.
Directed by Peter Rothstein.
(Photo by Sarah Whiting)

Some of the challenges of the theater are specific to the job; some are general to the profession. One common language, however, overlays all theatrical work, whether you are an actor, director, designer, producer, playwright, or any other of the tribe: theater people know how to speak hard work.

Costume designer Rich Hamson defines his own work in three ways: physical, psychological, and mental. "It's physical work, hard physical work; a large part of it is carrying stuff around. When you do small theaters, you're hauling in four or five bags of clothes all the time. Psychologically, it's hard work, because you have to end up being a psychiatrist for all these

Work, work, work. And after that, find more work.

—ACTOR RICARDO VAZQUEZ

Rich Hamson in the costume shop at Chanhassen Dinner Theatres, surrounded by dresses he designed for *Hairspray*. Hamson estimates that costume stock at Chanhassen is "easily" over three thousand costumes and many assorted pieces. (Photo by Emily Kopperud)

different people at once—a director, a choreographer, actors, people who are stitching for you." Being part of a close team can involve a high level of connection; encouraging, rewarding, and motivating are all part of the work. "Sometimes I think the hardest is the mental work," Hamson says. "When I'm doing a show, it's so hard for me to turn it off; it's always in my brain. It's in my brain when I wake up at night; I solve some of my best problems at three o'clock in the morning. To some extent you have to be obsessed with it in order to get it done."

Hard work, and decidedly tricky. The theater is a tremendous puzzle to put together. It does not always come together, and like any alchemy, even a slight shift in the ingredients can cause misfire. Sometimes, the makers have absolutely no idea why a show misses the mark—or everyone has a different idea—and this provides fodder for many passionate discussions and post-mortem free-for-alls. Those debates can be strongly anchored in the production itself or completely unmoored, since the artwork no longer exists to be experienced. You cannot go back, and even if you could, it would inevitably be different. A chief quality of the live theater is that it is ephemeral.

Joel Sass finds the ephemeral nature of theater to be "the most attractive and ruthless quality of the work. Even if you're running seven shows a week for six weeks, each experience is going to be unique. It's predicated on how the artists are that night with the material, walking the tightrope of the play in tandem with an audience which is always going to be different. Their composite makeup and what they bring to it, and the quality of their response has always been exciting to me. To the degree I'm theological at all, I think there's a holiness to it. There is something about that communal space, and sharing that story."

"But it's ruthless because it exists only in the memory of those who witnessed it and those who made it," Sass says. "I'm shocked at how quickly the recollection of that work and any physical evidence of it can decompose into the culture. Time is a meat grinder, you know? Even what seemed, to those who experienced it, to be a monumental artistic achievement, is reduced to shared anecdotes."

Sass calls the process "ruthless and appalling. On the other hand, that's the beauty of it. You can have three hundred people in a room, and they'll all walk away with such a highly individualized experience. It's theirs to cherish as long as they care to keep dusting it off on the mantle."

Penumbra co–artistic director Sarah Bellamy talks about the transience of live theater in another way. "Theater people practice seasons of life. We put everything we have into the creation of something that's only going to live for a little while, and then you're going to tear it down, and it will be gone. Only those people who are part of it, and the people who came to see it, will have known that being that was. And we practice these cycles of life and death perennially in the theater, over and over again. There's something amazing and brave about that."

Although any given day in the theater can seem unstructured, the arrangement of jobs can be quite stratified. Different job categories, if that is not too formal a term for the protean theater, require very different skill sets; the daily work of the sound designer is quite different from the daily work of the actor, which is quite different from the daily work of the producer or artistic director. It's the joining of all those different kinds of work that make the theater.

In practical terms, these different job skills offer many different entry points into theater work, and plenty of room in the hive for different kinds of people. In the same way that fortune favors the brave, the theater favors people with a big toolbox, as well as those who are willing to steer their own ships and have agency in their professional lives. Knowing where you want to go, and aiming there, is a plus in the theater, although such directionality is not universal. In career path terms, intentionality and steady progress are rather a rarity. Perhaps more than in other professions, people fall in, wander in, discover themselves in the theater; some are quite surprised to find themselves there. Still, many theater people recall an initial impulse or spark, a sense of finding a home in the polyglot theater, however winding the path that would ensue.

Joel Sass, who grew up in a town that didn't have live performance or

Don't make any plans; it's not a career you can plan. Live a serendipitous life: just take one thing at a time and work really hard. Do not turn down anything. And amass as many skills as possible.

—ACTOR BRADLEY GREENWALD

community theater, reminisced in an onstage conversation at the Guthrie that his theater interest started by "entertaining ourselves. The only thing we could really do was go out into a barn and become pirates for a week, or go down into a ditch to build a fort or a cabin. I was the bossy kid in the neighborhood who was always trying to conscript people and come up with the special effects. How to get the ship burning!"

Lighting designer Jesse Cogswell discovered in high school that his path would be in the theater. He remembers the moment when a technical theater teacher demonstrated a sequence he'd programmed into the school's new light board. The lights played along with the theme music from the movie *2001: A Space Odyssey*, the initial fanfare from Richard Strauss's *Thus Spake Zarathustra*. Cogswell thought it was "the coolest thing I'd ever seen."

Park Square artistic director Richard Cook was "totally seduced by theater" as a college student: "The whole field was of interest to me." Cook was recruited to be in the first class of the University of Iowa's master of fine arts program in theater and, years later, "became an artistic director by accident." His predecessor "handed me the keys sooner than we'd planned. And a shoebox full of bills. I'd never been trained for any of it."

Costume designer Rich Hamson also started out wanting to be an actor. After growing up in southern Minnesota, he moved to the Twin Cities and was living in a house with other young theater folk doing a season of summer stock (so called because scheduled productions rely on an inventory, a stock, of scenery and costumes, as opposed to building everything new). He recalls, "In one of the community shows I was doing, somebody else was doing the costumes and was having trouble with the chorus. It was the first time this happened, but I had a really clear picture in my head of what I thought it should look like. When you're twenty-two, you know everything, so I just went to the director and said, 'Well, you know, I could do your chorus costumes for you.'" Hamson had found a path.

Sound designer C. Andrew Mayer got his start in the field as a student at the conservatory at the old Children's Theatre Company and School. "I just walked into the sound booth in the fall and said, 'I'd like to run a show,'

Sound designer C. Andrew Mayer at work on cues for *Jericho* at the Minnesota Jewish Theatre Company. (Photo by C. Andrew Mayer)

and the guy went, 'Great.' And that was it. My whole life flowed from that moment. If he had said, 'Get out of here, you loser,' then my life would probably have been completely different."

Mayer took detours: through production management and film school. "I just had lucked into this incredibly fun and rewarding thing that I could do. Honestly, the dark secret truth about me is I never set out to be a sound designer in the theater. . . . It just so happened that I had this skill that I enjoyed doing, and I was getting paid for it; in the meantime, I'm trying to become a filmmaker or trying to travel the world. That's what I was really doing. And then suddenly you turn around and you're like, 'My god, this is how I'm making my living! How the hell did that happen?'"

Playwright Kira Obolensky entered through writing and the visual arts, particularly work with artists' books and fine presses. The first intern at the Minnesota Center for Book Arts, she also had a variety of other jobs. She recalls, "We had to pay bills, so I had a series of telemarketing jobs in my twenties. It was awful, but I was making money. It became harder and harder for me to get into the print shop and print studio. I was feeling really creatively frustrated. And the Playwrights' Center was here. I thought, well, I'd always written plays; I think I did it for Christmas, and the family. So I walked in the door and took a class and that's really how I became a playwright."

In 2014, the celebrated and much-awarded playwright Jeffrey Hatcher premiered a new play called *Jeffrey Hatcher's Hamlet*, recounting the tale of little Jeffrey directing a production with his fifth grade-class; his source material had been the Classics Illustrated comic book version of the play, with a cover featuring Hamlet being admonished by his father's ghost on the ramparts of Elsinore. For some reason, the ghost appears to be wearing sunglasses. Hatcher says his play is "about theater as a home, as a refuge, and as a platform." He found the experience of making a play to be addictive and "couldn't wait to replicate it." A life in the theater, born in a fifteen-cent comic book.

Actor H. Adam Harris was inspired as a young man by a production of *The Cherry Orchard* at the Classical Theatre of Harlem, saying, "Lightning struck, and I knew I wanted to do this for the rest of my life." Arriving in the Twin Cities to study at the University of Minnesota/Guthrie Theater BFA Actor Training Program for studies in the classical canon, Harris reached out beyond the core curriculum. He notes, "In this country, classical means male, white, and European, and so I was searching for myself in it. I typed into the university class search 'blacks plus theater' and a class popped up."

Harris found himself the sole African American male actor in a class called Blacks in American Theater. Lou Bellamy, the co–artistic director of St. Paul's Penumbra Theatre, admitted the young actor into his graduate-level class. Harris remembers, "I was getting all this training from the BFA program, but I was also in class with the master. My career has always been about the merger of this very classical world of theater and this black aesthetic, this black understanding of what it means to engage with life."

Set designer Kate Sutton-Johnson was "into chorus and acting and the visual arts" in high school. She went to North Carolina School of the Arts "guessing that I should go into scene painting or props or something like that, but not really understanding how you define those things or what those roles are. Very quickly some of the professors said, 'You're not in the right spot. You need to be in design.' I think they saw that I was an ideas person and that I would be a lot happier working in a conceptual part of the framework, rather than a craftsperson part of the framework."

When Jack Reuler founded Mixed Blood Theatre in 1976, he was just twenty-two years old. He says it has been his only job as a grown-up, and adds that it took him until about 2000 before he figured out, really, what his job was. "I started a theater that had a mission that was unlike any other. So I didn't have any real people to go to, to teach me in the world of nonprofit theater, or how to deal with race and culture in theater in new ways. I was always forging my own way. That's why I take so seriously trying to usher in the next generation of theater leaders, trying to impart some of the wisdom that it took me twenty-five years to gain. So they don't have to do everything by trial and error. I don't just have an occasional show that I lament; I have the 1980s!"

Not everyone comes to the theater as a first choice. Playwright Carlyle Brown had an entirely different career, as a captain of nineteenth-century sailing vessels, before he turned to the theater. Of drama, he recalls, "I was interested in this art form and, you know, the world of being at sea is a lot about stories; the sailor's craft about storytelling has kind of a decided purpose. I had this idea for a play; it was based on Shakespeare's *Othello* and consisted largely of the missing bedroom scenes in the play. It was ambitious for a first-time writer. It's New York, so you can just put an ad in the paper and find actors at your doorstep. I didn't go to school for theater so I had no idea what I was getting myself into. Well, it drove me broke and it drove me mad, and it was a disaster. I mean, a disaster. But I learned a lot, and I guess I had some addiction to that kind of madness."

Addiction and madness, possibly. Yet creative people continue to make that bargain, and to find their lives in the theater. For many, the rewards of theater work outweigh its disadvantages.

Jeremy Cohen, producing artistic director of the Playwrights' Center, puts it this way: "I'm the kind of artist who wants to go see things so that I can think, 'Oh my God, that's amazing!' I have to make art that's at least that good because it always keeps me on my toes. It always reminds me that it's a privilege that we're choosing a life which is a very passionate difficult life, and that we have the ability to be full and content in what we do, that we have great joy and pride in what we do."

"The rewards are more than compensation for making a life doing what you want to do," Jack Reuler says decidedly. "It's better to make less than to do something you don't love to do; that's where I think we really succeed. I don't know if making a living is about financial security and well-being. But it is about rewarded hearts and souls, doing what they love to do. Period."

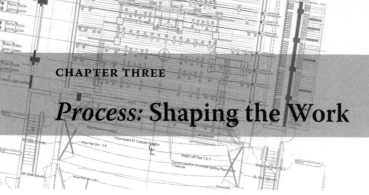

CHAPTER THREE

Process: Shaping the Work

Because dozens and sometimes hundreds of people are involved in the making of the artwork, a play on the stage is the end result of thousands of individual decisions, small and large, and all of them have a direct effect on the alchemy of creating a world on a stage and making it speak to an audience. That alchemy is complex, and it is exceedingly difficult to get right. In a sense, all decisions about *Chosen Play* are determinative, whether it is the casting of lead roles or the design of individual props. If there's a wrong note somewhere, the audience will feel it. Enough wrong notes and the entire effort will fall short. And, this being the theater, a decidedly presentational art form, everyone will know it.

As Soon as the Title Is Set for Production:
Assembling the Team

✓ *Writing the Play*	*Finding the Audience*
✓ *The Decision to Produce*	*Rehearsing*
✓ *Assembling the Team*	*Technical and Dress Rehearsals*
Casting the Show	*Opening Night*

Theater production involves specialists of many varieties, each of whom will have a strong influence on both the collaboration and its result. A team must be assembled: a director; designers for scenery, lighting, costumes, and sound; and, depending on the project, a music director and choreographer. In large theaters, and depending on the size of the show, add in assistants for some or all of the above. In small ones, for either aesthetic or practical reasons, some of these roles are combined into the work of one person; doubling or tripling jobs is not uncommon.

The work of the theater is messy, many-handed, impossibly ambitious, and full of high-profile personalities; it is also necessarily hierarchical. Without some kind of framework on which to hang the efforts of so many disparate workers, the wild creativity that is the hallmark of the best work would simply spill over, dissipate, and burn out.

For institutions and for seasons of work, the artistic director or artistic leader is at the top of the hierarchy, choosing the titles and setting overall vision. The apex for an individual play is occupied by a director, who is the person who will most strongly affect the execution of the play in all its complex aspects. The director is the boss, whose lead all the other people working on the show will try to follow (and to whom they will bring their questions). In naming the director for a particular project, the artistic director sets a course along which the production will sail, right through its closing night. Matching the director to the project is a vital skill for any artistic leader.

Who is the correct director for *Chosen Play*? Directors have styles— new work, the classics, musicals, Chekhov, Shakespeare, farce, comedy, contemporary drama. They have specialties—good with young actors, terrific with fight scenes, experienced with the complexities of the thrust stage or theater-in-the-round. Directors have inclinations—they like the Renaissance period but dislike nineteenth-century theater. They have aspirations—they always wanted to do this or that pet project, work with this actor or that designer, or perhaps try a style different from the one they're known for. They have schedules—booked up until next year, just had a project fall through and therefore available next month. And directors have careers—a particular project may be good for their growth as an artist, their reputation, or their bank account.

A directorial preparation and research period can last for many months, long before anyone else is giving a project serious thought. In fact, serious thought is the first part of the director's job. They read and study the play, along with its background, its period, its geography, and sometimes its production history. They think about it, long and hard. Before too long, troupes of designers, artisans, and actors will be counting on the director to guide their work both large scale and small. Time spent in study is a director's prep time, and will provide the basis for all the decisions shortly to be made, decisions which will need to be made faster and faster as the process speeds up. Research underlies the development of the creative vision for this particular production; prep time is the quiet beginning of what will eventually spring to life on opening night.

I'm happiest when I'm working. Even when I travel, I love to be traveling with research in mind. I just dig into the place I am in a deeper, richer way than just a relaxing vacation. I'm invigorated by the research process.

—ARTISTIC DIRECTOR PETER ROTHSTEIN

For a production of Tennessee Williams's *A Streetcar Named Desire*, director Randy Reyes began his research with the playwright. "I need to understand why the playwright wrote this play and what he was writing about. What about his life influenced this play. To me, it starts with the playwright. If I don't know that playwright's story, I'll never understand the actual play."

"Then you research the world of the play," Reyes continues, "so that we're making informed choices through the process in terms of design. I need to get the style and the idea. How do people treat each other? How did they interact during this time in the South? What does it mean if you're a doctor, or an alcoholic, during this time? You can't really get all that out of pictures; you need to read about the time."

Children's Theatre Company artistic director Peter Brosius has a method for adapting classic material, whether he is working on *The Jungle Book* or *The Wizard of Oz*. "You do your research. Why was it written, what was it about? What was the impact? What was its reception? What's core in that story, what's absolutely essential? You respect the source and investigate it as if you're doing it for the first time—because you *are* doing it for the first time."

In short, directors imagine an entire world and then go forward to place their own stamp on it. Then designers come to the table, imaginative energies ready, to create the physical world of *Chosen Play* through scenery and props; the air and atmosphere of the play through lighting design; the sound and music of the play's world through sound design and perhaps music direction; the look of the clothes, hair, and accessories through costume design. The leaders seek design colleagues whose artistic sensibilities are appropriate to *Chosen Play* and, not unimportantly, with whom they are willing to go through the stresses of the production process. Each member of the team is considered singly and in concert with the other likely participants. Have they worked together before? If so, how often? Does this past history matter?

"Often we find that we are continually in a mix of people that we know and have a history with, and people who are brand new to us," says Peter Brosius. Sometimes he specifically seeks artists with whom he has not worked before. "Is that easy?" he asks. "No, but the results are bracing. You're in a deep conversation, trying to find a shared language. . . . I'm continually hoping that there's a better idea than mine, that my team will challenge me. That work is the sum of all those energies and talents and it's pushed, prodded, critiqued, reimagined, and full of surprises. You have a lot of meetings; you sit around the table. And you just wrestle and wrestle and wrestle until it makes sense, until you find the right way to tell that story."

The Jungle Theater's Bain Boehlke, in contrast, typically works with the same community of artists that he has worked with for decades: "Working with people that I know allows us to understand what the bar is, the level of artistic achievement, or let's say the level of poetic veracity. I like to see truth on the stage."

Artists have good reasons for working together repeatedly over their careers. Understanding each person's aesthetic can be a strong predictor for cohesiveness in the final product, and longstanding teams can function like combat units in the battle to bring a play to the stage on time. They communicate in shorthand, they are familiar with each other's strengths

Randy Reyes *(center)* and company in Mu Performing Arts' production of *Into the Woods* at Park Square Theatre. Directed by Rick Shiomi. (Photo by Michal Daniel)

and shortcomings, and they can see the same aesthetic product off in the distance. Shared history breeds shared humor, an increasingly precious commodity as timelines shorten and workloads increase.

For Minnesota Playlist, Frank Theatre artistic director Wendy Knox wrote that her "incredible group of artists have truly made Frank what it is, and they are the main reason why we're still around. The posse around Frank (the artists and the boards) is a collection of smart, oddball, passionate, gifted folks; they will tackle the impossible, they will find a way, they will laugh their asses off while doing so, they will shake their heads in disbelief but rarely say 'no,' and they will come back for more."

Sometimes the director also works as the set designer, providing a cohesive vision between those two crucial roles. Boehlke, for one, designs all his own work. "In the American theater, the director is the painter of stage work, the one who organizes and marries all of the elements into a cohesive whole."

If designers can get along with the director and each other, and bring their own artistic vision to the process, can they also bring their part of the vision to fruition? Can they draft and draw? Can they work with the artisans and crew people effectively? Are they reasonable communicators? Do they understand the limitations, always present, of schedule and budget? Can they get in the boat with the others and row toward opening night?

As the team comes together, with design conversations that are first highly exploratory and later increasingly specific, creative exchange becomes the subterranean ongoing pulse of the project. Each designer also starts his or her own deep study of *Chosen Play* and its period, always seeking the right intersection between the artistic aspiration and the practical execution.

The scenic designer, early on, reads the play for what is required. What does *Chosen Play* need? Does it take place entirely in an open field? In a three-story house? Does it require six different settings, or ten, or two? How many entrances and exits will be needed? What are the paint requirements? Are there special effects—a trapdoor, an upper window, a rising moon, a rainstorm? What about furniture and set decoration? Are there likely to be fifty props, or one hundred and fifty? Are any of them trick props that must spin, or light up, or explode and burn? Critically, can everything be built in time and on budget and with the available shop resources? How will it all fit in the available stage space?

Set designer Kate Sutton-Johnson enjoys the early research work with the director. She finds that "that relationship is very special. I might intersect with the director before they have entirely decided what they think about the show, or about all the little dramaturgical things they're going to sort out. I like being a key participant in that. I love being part of that safe playing space where you sit without artwork and you talk about the project.

Maybe the next meeting you're looking at research and visual things to respond to. It's fun to have a hand in that."

The lighting designer studies the flow of scenes and the flow of time within them. What time of year does *Chosen Play* take place—bright summer, stark winter? What's the time of day, and what's the weather on those days? From what direction does the light come and in what color? How can the light support the mood of each moment and especially the most pivotal scenes? What are the places on the stage and set that need special lighting? How can the lights respond to the color and palette of the scenery and costume designs?

In addition, from a practical and highly technical perspective: does the performance space have enough lighting instruments and are they of the right kind to achieve these effects? What about the equipment to change the direction and color and combination of the lights? Will there be enough time after the set is installed, and before the actors arrive, to hang, focus, and adjust instruments that might number in the hundreds?

For the costume designer, in addition to researching the play, there's another set of information that must first be gathered and then given close consideration. A major element of her work—the actors—is entirely unavailable until later, sometimes much later in the process, when casting is announced. Costumes are built onto bodies. They are worn by actors, and the wise costume designer keeps the thought of the individual actor in his toolbox, along with historical research, a strong sense of color and design, and his sketchpads. Can this particular actor handle long skirts? What is her body type? Can he or she, if required, wear practically nothing and still look good?

Moreover, what is the period of *Chosen Play*? Is it full of complex Elizabethan clothes or a simpler beatnik style? How many characters are there? How many times does each of them change clothes? How many garments will be needed? What about shoes? Hats? Wigs? Facial hair? Does any of this exist in costume storage in the relevant theater? Is any of it rentable? If so, are those garments the right size for this particular actor? Are they the right color to go with the palette of scenery, lights, and the rest of the show? Does the director want, for aesthetic purposes, an entire scene to be in a particular color? Each body is unique, each character is unique, each piece of clothing will have both an aesthetic impact and a practical one. Costume construction, or even assemblage, takes time. Tremendous amounts of material and intensive labor are involved, even before considering how all the clothes will be organized, stored, cleaned, and maintained.

Costume designer Sonya Berlovitz starts with the script: "As I'm reading, I always get images swimming through my brain automatically. So that's a part of what I first start to put down on paper. I sketch. I'm a naturally curious person, so I look at magazines, newspapers, film, things that inspire me. It's all food for thought." At design meetings, Berlovitz admits, she is usually nervous, even after so many years in the business; yet, "I like that moment where you are taking a risk and putting your ideas out there. I find that very invigorating as an artist. It's very motivating."

While considering and studying all these matters for *Chosen Play*, the designers and the director are almost certainly doing other projects at other stages of the production process: development, rehearsals, technical rehearsals. Sound designer C. Andrew Mayer recalls a recent year when, between September and May, he worked on sixteen separate projects. "They're never nicely spaced out," he says, remembering five or six solid weeks of technical rehearsal, with no days off. "I'm pretty sure I'm the busiest person in town." Freelancers jump from theater to theater and sometimes from city to city, doing shows and moving on. A considerable amount of the work in the American theater is done on airplanes and in hotel rooms.

A Year (or So) Before Opening Night: Casting the Show

✓ *Writing the Play*	*Finding the Audience*
✓ *The Decision to Produce*	*Rehearsing*
✓ *Assembling the Team*	*Technical and Dress Rehearsals*
✓ *Casting the Show*	*Opening Night*

Twelve months out from opening night for *Chosen Play* (less for some theaters), some key pieces are set. Rough dates are in place for the build, for the rehearsals, for the performances, for the announcing and marketing. The budgets set by the producer and presented to the designers are under review and challenge. Whatever the size of the theater or its budget, there is always pressure to stretch, to do as much as can be done. The director and designers are talking with some frequency; the designers are meeting with each other. Each of these creators is assailed by the practical—will there be time and money to build the show the way they intend?—and each is intently hanging on to the vision under that assault. Their design meetings are long and discursive and often a kind of haven from the practical. During these meetings, designers meld their visions together, brainstorm solutions for problems that might have seemed intractable, and listen closely to the director, who is trying to bring all the visions together into one cohesive production.

The world of *Chosen Play* is taking shape. Now it must be populated.

When it comes time to find these bodies to populate the play, you can be sure that a large number and wide range of actors—of every stripe, persuasion, age, disposition, and experience level—will want to be in the production. All actors passionately want to be on stage and, at any given moment in time, the majority of them are out of work. Open your window and call out that you are casting *Chosen Play*, and you will hear the rush of many feet moving toward the sound of your voice. They are accelerating. Better close that window.

Theaters that are associated with Actors' Equity Association (the actor's union) are required to hold general auditions every year. Theaters that do not have agreements with Equity cast more intermittently and perhaps by individual show, according to the roles needed at that particular time. Most theater directors have a working familiarity with a group of actors, whether through previous use or seeing their work on stage elsewhere. If they are visiting in town, they will rely on theater staff for advice.

All auditions are intended as a method for actors to show their wares to producing organizations, who may then be interested in calling them back for a second or third look. The process is inherently brutal; there are many candidates and only one role.

Twin Cities actor Nathaniel Fuller auditioned for the Guthrie Theater for ten years "on and off" without success. Each audition received a version of the "very good, thank you" response, which, he says, translates into "don't call us and we won't call you." Here is his story of the audition that brought him into the Guthrie company:

> I decided that if I had to keep going through this process, I was going to do it as much for me as for them. I wanted to have a little fun and maybe create a bit of a surprise. Garland Wright was casting *Richard III* and I had an opportunity to audition for him. This is how I introduced my monologue: "My next piece is classical," I said. "It's Shakespeare. What you are about to see is an experiment to test Stanislavski's theory that there are no small parts. What follows are some dozen or so roles I'd most likely be cast in my first year in a major repertory company."
>
> I then turned my back on Mr. Wright, walked away a few steps, wheeled and shouted, "Arm! Arm! The enemy doth make assault!" I turned away again, turned back and went through a series of thirteen Shakespearean messenger and servant speeches in a variety of over-the-top characterizations and scenery-chewing accents. . . . I entered a palace and silently passed from hope to horror to despair before uttering an abject, "I will, my liege," and departing. The moving Birnam Wood was described to the Scottish king in the thickest throat-tangling brogue I could muster. I tersely informed Brutus of his wife

Longtime Guthrie actor Nathaniel Fuller.
(Photo courtesy of Nat Fuller)

Fulvia's death. Frantically and manically I screamed to Lady Cap-
ulet of the chaos in her kitchen. I hissed a warning to Caesar of
dangerous portents in the entrails of a beast.

Finally, I ran into a mob-filled street shouting for "Jack Cade!
Jack Cade!" With a sudden grunt I arched sharply back from a
sword blade in my back, doubled forward with a groan from a
thrust to the guts, and, wheezing, collapsed to sitting on my rear.
With a look of pain and bewilderment I began to gurgle. Slowly,
slowly, I toppled sideways into a contorted, sprawling, open-eyed
demise concluded by the inevitable drawn-out death rattle.

Fuller was hired. The audition he describes was in 1988; he still works
regularly at the Guthrie.

Actors have only a few minutes to present at auditions; the stakes are
high and conditions are rarely perfect. They are having a day like everyone
else is having a day, and it might have included a car that wouldn't start, a
night without sleep, a head cold, or something worse. None of that matters;
each actor still has just three minutes to show the best that he or she can
do, and to demonstrate his or her versatility.

When Ricardo Vazquez was finishing up at the University of Minnesota/
Guthrie Theater BFA Actor Training program in 2007, he participated in a
series of auditions, hoping that one would lead to a job. Artistic directors
from the Twin Cities and from elsewhere came to see the about-to-be-
minted BFAs. Vazquez recalls, "We had maybe thirteen or fourteen different artistic directors come in and audition us. By fourteen of these, I

*Figure out what's unique about you, what you do that other people
don't do. And say yes. There are lots of different ways to participate
creatively in the world. Don't say no. Say yes.*

—PLAYWRIGHT KIRA OBOLENSKY

hadn't received anything. Literally the last person to come through was from the Hudson Valley Shakespeare Festival in New York. He called me back, which was a sign that he was interested. I was doing the Romeo monologue at the time, and I did it as I'd been trained. And he said, 'Okay. Now I want you to do that monologue again, but do it as though you're being attacked with a BB gun.'"

Vazquez obliged, "had a great time," and was given another challenge. On his résumé he had listed Mickey Mouse as a special skill; no one had ever asked for it. The artistic director, however, now asked him to do a Mickey Mouse monologue, picking the most inappropriate one possible for Mickey. Vazquez was ready: "I had a David Mamet monologue in my back pocket, so suddenly Mickey was doing Mamet for him, and he loved it. A couple of days later, I got a call asking if I wanted to join that company."

Auditioning, Vazquez says now, is "a necessity, a resource, and a tool. Every single actor has to get used to it, because that is the only way that you're ever going to get work. And even when you think that everybody has seen your work and should know what you do, you'll be asked to audition again. You have to go in there as if no one has ever seen you and let them know that you can still do fresh work."

Nonetheless, auditions are not always the best indication of an actor's potential. Some actors are good at auditioning, and others are not. It's generally agreed that the best way for a director or artistic director to get a sense of an actor's real work and range is to see her in a play, which is the end result of a process of study and rehearsal that mirrors to some degree the process for any production.

John Miller-Stephany was associate artistic director of the Guthrie Theater from 1999 to 2015, seeing, on average, four local productions per week. He reflects, "Part of what we did institutionally was to get to know Twin Cities actors in terms of their work beyond a ten-minute audition appointment. Seeing actors in performance is a far better way to assess their abilities."

During those years, Miller-Stephany adds, the Guthrie generally started each casting process locally, before widening the search to include out-of-town actors. "Whenever possible, our policy was to conduct local audi-

Director John Miller-Stephany in the Guthrie Theater rehearsal room with actor Stacia Rice for a production of *Jane Eyre.* (Photo by Michal Daniel)

tions first and see how much of the casting we could do in Minneapolis–St. Paul. The idea was to give local actors first consideration; that was for philosophical reasons as well as financial ones. The Guthrie was founded and flourishes because of the good graces of the people of the Twin Cities community; if there's a local artist who could play the role to the director and producer's satisfaction, we felt that we owed it to the community to support local talent." In the 2013–14 season, Miller-Stephany notes, the Guthrie hired ninety-eight actors over the course of the year and eighty-three of them were based in the Twin Cities.

But, of course and inevitably, not everyone is working at the time *Chosen Play* is being cast. And no one can see all actors in all plays; in the Twin Cities alone, there are dozens of professional and semiprofessional stages operating at any given time. Sometimes auditions plus résumés and head shots are the only way.

One of the glories and the constrictions of the acting profession is the plain fact that the actor's body is his or her instrument and, in the live theater, the body is the inescapable house for the character. Costumes and stage tricks aside, an actor may have all the talent and craft a role requires but may also be too tall, too short, too old, too young, the wrong body shape, or something more subtle. It isn't enough for the director or casting person to think someone *can* do the part. The casting person has to think that actor is *right* for the part, and not just the part on the page but the character the director is envisioning for the particular production.

When those who are casting don't know an actor's work, even with all their skill and experience and ability to recognize talent, there is a risk. It is very difficult to judge how an actor will go through the rigors of rehearsal, and whether that actor will come out on the other side as the character envisioned.

Casting is an alchemical process and, like all alchemies, it has compounds and catalysts. Some actors astound and surprise with the depth of their work. They bring dimensions to their characters, and to the play, that the director never imagined. These actors become essential to the vision, deepening it, taking it far beyond where the director had thought it could go. The challenge, and the skill, is to recognize which are those actors.

A director can choose only a small percentage of the actors seen, and an even smaller percentage of those who want to be seen. The office or study wall is covered with head shots and sticky notes, continually grouped and regrouped. The director locks down the actors one by one, approaching the inevitable compromises with resolution and the beautiful surprises with gratitude. Job offers are made and accepted; the production's company is set.

Six to Eight Months Before Opening Night:
Finding the Audience

✓ *Writing the Play* ✓ *Finding the Audience*
✓ *The Decision to Produce* *Rehearsing*
✓ *Assembling the Team* *Technical and Dress Rehearsals*
✓ *Casting the Show* *Opening Night*

Money is being spent on *Chosen Play*. House costs are ongoing: the rent, the heat, the overhead, the staff. Show costs are on the horizon and in closer view: fees for artists, script costs, materials to build the sets and costumes, people to use the materials. Attention must be paid. In the commercial theater, the intention is to make money. In the nonprofit theater, the intention is . . . to make money, which then will be plowed back into the organization. Barring grants and donations, making money means filling the house and holding, as closely as possible, to early speculative calculations about the costs of the show.

By six to eight months before opening night, projections about the audience become a crucial part of the calculation. The management team considers matters that need discussion and resolution: How many people will see the show, and at what ticket prices? Will we offer discounts—for groups, for seniors, for students—and how will that affect the bottom line? Will we buy advertising? Where will it appear? Print? Online? Posters, mailings, flyers, billboards, bus stop posters? Email lists and list-serves? Public transit vehicles? On television or radio? Will we promote the show on social media? What visual images will we use to promote the show? (Although some actors have been contracted at this point, costumes have yet to be built. How, then, will we obtain the crisp punchy photographs that all this promotion will need to be successful?)

The making of the marketing and communication plan is, in many ways, as complex as the making of *Chosen Play*, and no less critical to the theater's future. In the best cases, the two work in harmony to find the audience and bring them in the doors.

Every play needs to distinguish itself in the crowded entertainment market of today. If a show runs eight times per week in a 200-seat house for three weeks, for example, that's 4,800 seats to fill, and very little time for word of mouth to take effect. Like airplane seats, every one that goes unfilled is lost revenue. Lost revenue weighs heavily against not only the bottom line but also the production's intention, which is to fill up the house. The theater requires an audience.

Artistic director Richard Cook defines his Park Square Theatre as a place where "we support the talent with worthwhile material, strong directors, smart designers, and I think as importantly as anything, there's always an audience in the house. It's so frustrating to have put so much heart, soul, thought, intelligence, resources, and energy into a performance and then have three people in the house. That's not what any of us set out to do." The job of marketing, as Cook notes, is to get the right audience for this group of artists into the room at the same time. "If that's not happening," he says, "then the theater is not doing its job."

Better get with a media plan. *Chosen Play* is going to be competing for the attention of feature writers, columnists, television producers, radio personalities, and bloggers. Theater critics and arts writers from the dailies, the weeklies, the neighborhood papers, and the electronic media must be informed, if not wooed.

All those who are associated with selling tickets to the show—the producers and promoters and press representatives—face a series of tough assignments less lustrous than the task of bringing the play to the stage. They have to know the potential audience and figure out a way to translate the experience of *Chosen Play* into a language that will lure people into buying tickets. Marketers and promoters have to know how the public will react to a familiar title. If it's a new script, they sometimes need to translate it before it has ever been on a stage. With any play, new or not, the message has to reflect, alluringly, something that does not yet exist.

As the whole production team speeds toward the opening of *Chosen Play*, hard cash is being spent. In the rushing and the artistic excitement, which, one hopes, is still the driving force, it can be possible to forget that, soon, just as much money needs to be taken in—or better yet, more.

The economic realities of the theater can be brutal. A large percentage of most budgets is spent on people; that is an appropriate assignment of resources in a line of work that is human-driven, human-performed, and human-oriented. But in cash-flow terms, many of the dollars necessary to mount a show are spent and gone before there's even a possibility of revenue, and the spending only increases as preproduction time goes on.

The University of Minnesota's Department of Theatre Arts and Dance, in addition to its academic year theaters and productions, operates a summer season on the Minnesota Centennial Showboat that floats on the Mississippi River. The vagaries of university budgeting mean that the showboat season is accounted for completely separately from its institutional house, and, consequently, the Minnesota Centennial Showboat, operated with plays of similar styles since 1958, can be considered an example of a good-sized show mounted as a freestanding effort, planned for a predicted run, in predictable conditions. All those predictions were rendered irrelevant in the summer of 2014, when a historic flood struck the Mississippi. The theater opened and closed on the same night in June, because the river was rising so rapidly there was no assurance that anyone would be able to get to the boat the next day. The showboat remained closed for nineteen of its planned sixty-two performances, until the flood had run its course.

Quite suddenly, and with no predictable outcome, the entire financial structure of the season was in ruins. The costumes and scenery had been built and installed in the theater. The director and artistic staff had been hired and done their work; rehearsals had happened. Marketing and promotion buys had been made. Some tickets had been presold, but against those months of expenses, only one night's revenue—the opening night—could be counted. Extensive television coverage of the flood featured aerial footage of a picturesque Minnesota Centennial Showboat marooned by water. No momentum could be established, no word of mouth. Only a short extension of the run could be contemplated, as actors had other obligations (school). In this case, once the flood subsided and the theater was able to reopen, through heroic staff efforts, the buoyancy of the actors, and the loyalty of the audience, the theater fought back to break even.

In the last months before a production opens, it must be physically prepared and installed in the performance space. Scenic and costume designs go into the shop, to the skilled ministrations of carpenters, painters, tailors and stitchers, milliners, prop-builders, and a horde of other specialists who will take the design ideas off the page and into three dimensions. Materials still need to be bought, and schedules and payrolls need to be met. Promotional campaigns must be planned, with the requisite expenditures for graphics and advertising. There may be season ticket revenue. There may be presales. But the cash flow is largely outgoing until the audience arrives.

Momentum is discernible and the pace is increasing. And then, in the midst of all the effort and flurry, one of the best days in the theater arrives to kick the process into another gear: the actors come to work.

CHAPTER FOUR

The Nature of Theater People

They are the books, the arts, the academes,
That show, contain and nourish all the world.
　　　　　—William Shakespeare, *Love's Labour's Lost*

From a bird's-eye view, the Twin Cities theater community could be said to resemble a many-celled organism whose shape is widespread and constantly shifting. If it were possible to perch on a cloud above the metro area in the several hours before curtain, say in October or November when the show season is in full swing, it might also be possible to use a good strong follow spot with a very long beam to bring theater folk into focus as they go about their business. Think Scrooge swooping through the air courtesy of the Ghost of Christmas Present and viewing people below; here are some things that would be seen.

Dozens of theaters are operating tonight and are about to click over from their workaday, not-always-beautiful selves into the playhouses where all the little worlds of all the plays will be presented. Some are large, some small, and some miniscule. From our cloud perch, consider those playhouses as points of light against the darkening Upper Midwest landscape; sundown is well behind by curtain time in the Twin Cities by mid-autumn. Who are the people going to work?

All over town, actors are picking up their actor bags, complete with bottles of water, and leaving their apartments and homes, getting in their cars or on buses. Theater folk with children are catching a quick supper with the kids before heading off to work, leaving them with spouses or family or babysitters. Several carloads of actors have loaded up and are driving out of the city toward Chanhassen Dinner Theatres for the evening show. They make the half-hour's drive six days a week in all kinds of weather; on two-show days they just stay out there between shows. They know the route well.

Everyone working tonight is starting to think about the show. Some show is opening; those people are exhilarated. Some show is closing; those people, some of them, are afraid they will never work again.

In the theaters, box office staffs are checking their will-call files, and some are putting out signage to direct patrons to the rush lines. In some theaters, phones are ringing; people are still calling to buy tickets for tonight's show, and that is always good news.

In various backstages, run crews are arriving to ready the stage house—above, below, behind, and to the sides of the stage proper—for the show. Someone is walking onto a dark stage and carrying off the ghost light, clicking it off until it is needed again. Someone turns on the work lights, which mercilessly flood the stage and backstage; it might be dirty in the corners. Magical atmospheric light will come later. The light board operator is firing up the board and running through preshow checks, instrument by instrument, making sure the focus is holding and the lamp and color are still good. The deck crew tests the traps—the trapdoors—and any and all moving scenery, then sweeps and mops the stage floor to a pristine condition. It is briefly deafening in the house while the sound crew runs their favorite loud music through the system, listening to each speaker in turn. And then it is relatively quiet, just a workplace getting ready to come alive.

Below stage, or behind it, in dressing rooms that are sometimes cramped and dark, the wardrobe people are checking costumes, ironing or starching as necessary, checking to make sure the previous night's notes ("hem coming loose on red dress," "my boots are falling apart!") are taken care of. And clothes are being counted; have all the clean socks and "skins" (underwear) come out of the laundry and been returned to dressing rooms?

Somewhere in town, almost certainly, there is a quick rehearsal—a pickup—for a company that has been dark for a few days and wants to refresh its rhythm. And somewhere there is an understudy rehearsal. Someone cannot perform; the understudy is reviewing the role and, depending on his or her degree of previous preparation, is exhilarated or terrified. The stage manager and a dresser are scrambling to see if the costumes made for the principal actor will also fit the understudy.

There's probably a fight call at one or two theaters—fights are run through every night to ensure that they are properly routined and that they are not as dangerous as they look. If any of the fighters felt a little out of rhythm during the previous show, or if any of the weapons seemed to get a little too close, the fight choreographer will be taking a rigorous look.

On several stages, the dance captain is checking positioning and calling counts. On some stages, or below them, musicians are arriving with their cased instruments, with or without tuxes and concert dress.

On more than one of these stages, a solitary actor is moving through her pattern, thinking about how to make a comedy moment funnier, a story moment more poignant, a tragic moment more effective. And in various small lounges, or greenrooms, actors and crew grab coffee, glance at the callboard, and sit for a minute to say hello before going on to their preparations.

Stage managers are already at their post (omnipotence is a more than full-time job), and their early arrival hour is sometimes their only relatively peaceful moment of the night. They have fixes—all the little things from last night's show that can be tweaked to improve it—and will soon start making the rounds to dressing rooms and to crew to deliver notes and attend to any problems. Periodically, the stage manager checks the callboard sign-in sheet, which also carries a note about anything special about this performance: perhaps a post-show discussion with the audience, or an ASL interpreter. Someone has posted a cartoon of some kind.

In theaters with multiple stages playing, this pattern of preparation doubles or triples.

In some theaters, a separate set of people working on a different show is working in the rehearsal room while the playing show occupies the stage. Rehearsal furniture, standing in for furniture being sought or built, stands on a taped-out floor exactly the same size as the stage. Rehearsal costumes hang on a rack. On a battered chaise longue, an actor reads a script.

If it's October, a number of holiday shows are certainly in rehearsal.

Dickens's *A Christmas Carol*, ever green in all its many variations, will be providing its usual welcome full houses for a set of theaters. The Guthrie's version is rehearsing tonight, with many actors returning to a play and a process very familiar to them and beloved by Twin Citians. By the time the annual production closes, right around December 25, the actors and company will have spent hundreds of hours and some fifty performances together. Some theatrical families are cast together in the show, and they make it the centerpiece of their own holidays. To celebrate the season, the company will take part in more than the usual number of backstage rituals: the Secret Santa, and the Adopt-a-Family charity project with its Jammie Breakfast and its gift-wrapping party with chili cook-off.

All over the residential neighborhoods in the Twin Cities, someone who is wishing they were rehearsing or performing tonight is putting on their hipster clothes to go see a friend on stage. Directors and designers are not on show calls, having been released from their contracts on opening night. From our high-cloud vantage point, we can still see them, working in their offices or homes or in coffee shops. They are researching or networking with colleagues. They might be settled deep in a chair, reading background on the cultural history of the period of their next show. They might be listening to music, looking for the right aural background to open an upcoming project. They might be poring over head shots, trying to figure out how to direct a big-cast show on a small-cast budget.

Somewhere in this landscape, production meetings are taking place, with groups of theater people sitting intensely around tables, scrutinizing scripts and set models and costume sketches. These meetings are often lengthy, sometimes contentious, always absorbing.

In either downtown Minneapolis or St. Paul, or both, members of a road show company are leaving their hotel rooms and heading for one of the big presenting houses, the State or Orpheum Theatres or the Ordway; these folks have been on the road for weeks or months in a touring show produced elsewhere and presented here. Maybe after the show tonight they'll try a new bar. No matter how curious they are about the Twin Cities theater community, they'll likely not see any local work while they're in town since they are on exactly the same work schedule.

In dressing rooms all over town, whether comfortable or sparse, early arriving actors are going through personal preshow rituals that may be quite complex. They warm up vocally and physically. They review their own notes from the previous performance. They might walk through the auditorium or stay strictly out of it. Their dressing tables might be covered with totems or mementos, or completely clean and clear. They greet each other and the dressers who, in bigger theaters, come in with clean laundry and freshly pressed costumes.

In a few theaters, actors are preparing for major physical transformations into full-body costumes or elaborate makeup. Extra time in the dressing-room chair may be required. Since the actor's body is his toolbox, care must be taken not to restrict or confine it too much, particularly the expressive face.

In the few hours before the show begins, time is inexorable, but it has one hard marker. The level of formality can vary, but thirty minutes before curtain, the stage manager starts calls: "Ladies and gentlemen, this is your half-hour call. Half-hour, please."

Everything accelerates. Everything slows down. And at about the same time, another call brings it all home by marking the arrival of the last and perhaps most important component of this complex mechanism: "House is open, ladies and gentlemen. House is open." The audience is arriving. From our perch on the cloud, we see them, many hundreds of them, driving away from their homes and toward the glowing theaters, walking out of their individual lives into the collective experience of live performance. As they pass through the lobbies, shedding their coats, they form a new, if temporary, organism. They will, we hope, laugh together, be moved together, in an experience that is simply, radically, entirely different from being entertained in solitude, or even collectively by a transmission through a screen.

The stage manager checks the sign-in sheet one more time to be sure all actors are in the house. Lights are now in the preset mode—whatever the designer has chosen as the initial impression for the audience. Houselights are up. The stage gleams. Onstage props and furniture are all set; no more running center to give something a last-minute check. Prop tables offstage are perfectly placed and waiting. Stashed in the backstage are meticulously arranged piles of costumes, set for quick changes, bodices open, shoes unlaced, cravats and neckwear prepped with secret elastic. In the dressing rooms, actors are donning their costumes, fixing their wigs, finishing their makeup, about to transform themselves into their characters. Crew folk have changed out of their workaday clothes and into their blacks, the better to be invisible in the backstage. They are going to their opening spots and checking their headset communication with the stage manager, who is headed for the control booth, prompt book in hand; the fifteen, the five, and the places calls will happen from there. Light board operators and perhaps sound operators are probably up there, as well, or soon will be, relaxing. If glass or plexiglass encloses the booth, they chat. If there is no audio barrier, they sit quietly, perhaps listening to the nearby audience members. Those in the booth look out at the audience; they don't need to count the house. They perceive it as light, half, good, full, or packed. Out front, the house manager is troubleshooting and ushers are handing out programs and smiling at patrons. Anticipation is in the air.

At this moment, the moment before the play begins, there's a place for everything and everything is in its place. It's a moment of intense collective concentration, centered on the most important place in the theater. The intersection between the stage light and the darkness of the backstage, the sightline, is clearly defined and impenetrable, but not for long. The world of the play, as yet still and uninhabited, is waiting on stage for the moment of ignition.

Everyone in the backstage is aware of the audience. There's nearly always a house system that lets actors hear the progress of the play from their dressing rooms, ostensibly to hear their cues. But the attentive ear can also hear the audience coming in—rustling and chatting, putting their coats down, opening their programs.

"Places" is called. Out front, ushers close the doors and close out the world. From the booth, the stage manager takes a breath and says, "House to half, go." The lights begin to dim. People settle further into their seats and stop talking. They turn their faces to the stage. "House out, go." The lights go out. When they come back, the world of the play begins to spin;

the collective work of actors, directors, designers, artisans, crew—all the theater workers—goes on display.

Theater is a life on the edge. Why do so many people put themselves through this? Why would anybody be drawn to this art, an art that is aspirational and sometimes, despite a formidable collection of talent and effort, simply fails? Hundreds of theater folk are doing their work on any given show night in the Twin Cities, a merry band of brigands living this tenuous existence. Are you one of them?

You might belong in the theater if you relish . . .

. . . problem solving, all day and every day.

The theater presents an unending series of challenges. Making art, or even good theater, with a group of opinionated humans is not a fluid process. It is chaotic. Are you familiar with the Japanese video game Katamari? A magical, highly adhesive ball, which keeps increasing in speed, picks up objects of all sizes as it rolls over them in its landscape. They then protrude from the ball's surface and continually change its direction. Theater work is like that ball: you have to keep up, and the path is always changing.

. . . doing all that problem solving at high speed.

The show, as they say, must go on. And it must go on without stopping. As stage manager Chris Code relates, "We spend a good deal of time worrying in a constructive manner about how we can be prepared for the bad stuff that can happen. Walls have fallen down on stage. People don't make their entrances. Props get lost, hats get misplaced. That's where I draw the real gratification of the job—fixing the problems. Being a spontaneous troubleshooter. When things are going wrong and you're in the hot seat, you're the one that people look to for the answers, as in, 'What are we going to do now?' It's a live show. People are expecting to see that person walk on stage or go through that door that suddenly won't open, or use that piece of scenery that isn't there. To successfully figure those things out and make the show work night after night is immensely personally gratifying to me."

. . . periodic, even regular, crises.

Excitement is always in the air, and internal combustion is a necessary part of the engine. Some theater folk have what might be called high-profile personalities; all are opinionated and passionate about what they do. They care. The work takes place in a crucible; pressure increases. Boom. Crisis survival and the ability to put crisis behind you is necessary for all.

Set designer Kate Sutton-Johnson remarks, "I definitely think I'm a sucker for the intensity. I love tech. I love just doing nothing but being at work for eighteen hours and then doing it all over again the next day. What happens in that space in time with just those people; I just get a lot out of it."

Sometimes you'll have a challenge in front of you, and you're either going to deal with it or it's going to get you.

—DESIGNER MARCUS DILLIARD

. . . working in real time and on a hard deadline.

From the first moment company members start to work on a play, they can hear the audience coming. The half-hour call will come. The first preview will come. No escape and no delay; they are coming.

"We need deadlines," says Bonnie Morris of the Illusion Theater. "The show opens. In a lot of other businesses, you get another week or three more weeks or something. We get it done. We do it and then we deliver. You can't be a procrastinator when you're in the theater, or at least there's a limit to how much you can procrastinate."

As lighting designer Jesse Cogswell says, "All your work is done in front of people, at the very last minute. They're not going to push the opening day back because you're not ready."

. . . taking a flier.

Because each piece of theater, and in fact each live performance, is a brand-new piece of construction, never the same, it also presents a set of challenges that have never been solved before. As a young designer, Marcus Dilliard was once asked to build a theater inside a ballroom. "I had no experience in that at that time," he says. "It's one of those situations where you say, 'Yeah, I can do that.' And then you go home and you figure out what you need to know in order to do it."

. . . attempting to make order from chaos.

All theater work might be called purposeful chaos, but on the first day of the technical and dress rehearsals, chaos is evident and clear. Complex technical systems are overlaid on the structure of the play. Carefully laid plans either demonstrate their efficacy or are tossed and remade. This can include hundreds of lighting instruments of various kinds, miles of cabling, quantities of colored gels, equipment and speakers, actual scenery and furniture (sometimes with unanticipated size or heft), show props (sometimes with the paint still wet), costumes, wigs and hairpieces, show shoes. Every physical element of the play must be assessed, tested, and made to take its proper place. It is both bewildering and wonderful when the elements are all there to be shaped and used by actors, directors, and designers. Order, and possibly art, out of chaos.

. . . multitasking.

Because there are always more tasks than can be accomplished, theater people are always doing more than one thing at a time. Managing and prioritizing work lists is an especially critical skill for designers, artisans, and stage managers.

. . . life that is episodic, with well-defined markers and with occasional long periods away.

The rhythm of theater work has projects with strongly defined beginnings and endings; sometimes there are weeks or months between projects. Playwright Kira Obolensky says she has "been through very fertile, very creative periods where I've actually generated an enormous amount of work. And then I'm fallow for a couple of years, and then things get fertile again." Actor Anna Sundberg feels that her downtime is fruitful, too. "Sometimes my favorite part about working is not working. It's very fertile. I love to work but it's all-encompassing. It's just nice to put it away."

... making and keeping relationships that overlap workplace and life.

Having the ability and desire to make relationships is critical to functioning as part of this complicated amoeba community. It's a schmooz-ocracy. Someone who's an intern now may, next season, be running a new theater and have jobs to give out.

"In the theater," director Peter Rothstein explains, "you build the lasting relationships by working together. That's the key. Until you work together, you're just acquaintances, and when you work together, you really become colleagues and friends in so many ways."

Theater people are renowned for picking up genuine friendships after years and decades of not seeing each other. Time in the trenches is rarely forgotten; bonds forged in the crucible are readily accessible throughout life. Theater relationships lie somewhere between workplace friendships and the best friendships one will ever have. The theater is intense and can be the most solidly built framework of one's life.

Michael Robins of the Illusion Theater puts it this way: "We're constantly forming, bonding fast, and then going away. Something's over and you have to go on to the next thing." He chuckles, "In the work we're in, there's always the excitement of the courtship, falling in love, wrestling with that, and then it's over."

... (perhaps most importantly) people and the way they tick.

The theater has room for the misanthrope, who can sometimes be found toiling in solitude in a corner. But the generative act of the theater is to re-create the world, and that requires close attention and a lively interest in the way it works. "You have to be a curious person," notes artistic director Randy Reyes, "and you have to love humanity. You're telling their story. Because you are human, you represent humanity, and I think it's your responsibility to do that with unrelenting pursuit of truth.'"

You might belong in the theater if you can thrive in an atmosphere of . . .

. . . keeping at it until it's brilliant.

Playwright Aditi Kapil reflects on writing plays: "It's never ever brilliant the first time out. You have to have your center and know how to filter all the noise into the thing that is useful to you as a generative artist. And hanging on to that like crazy. Because no one wants your mediocre work, no one wants your crappy work, no one even wants your great work. They want your brilliant work. The reason it takes me three years is because that's how long it takes for it to be something so magical that I'm okay with it being in print." The same impulses apply for directors, actors, designers, and others.

Develop your own taste through voracious intake of art. Aspire to create what you most want to see in the theater right now, and then try to make that. Don't quit until your artistry is equal to your imagination. And don't be afraid to fail a lot.

— PLAYWRIGHT, ACTOR, AND DIRECTOR ADITI KAPIL

. . . dysfunction, stress, and compulsion.

Here are some things often encountered in the theater: dilettantes, childlike behavior, destructive acting out, tirades, blinding egos. All are exacerbated by fatigue and pressure. Director Rick Shiomi says, "Theater is like a drug, in a sense. A habit, a compulsive habit. Nobody in their right mind would do it."

Also often encountered: daily invention on a scale that staggers, as well as genius, some of which may be one's own.

Sound designer C. Andrew Mayer: "We work together in such intense environments. Every theater develops its own sort of peculiar dysfunction, familial style dysfunction, which is why it's good to freelance, because you can sort of skip over the surface of that stuff. So somebody who can come in and be cheerful and get the work done without bringing negative energy into the room is really valuable. And for Minnesotans, this Minnesota nice thing is important. It's culturally pervasive at all these theaters; no matter how good your work, if you're a jerk to work with, it won't last."

. . . uncertainty and gradual decision making.

Despite the ticking clock and the demands of the process and of colleagues, the best solutions sometimes have to ripen in order to be revealed. Everyone may need the answer in order to proceed with their own work, yet it might still be best to wait. Willingness to wait for the right answer is a particularly good quality for designers and directors. It's still not easy, though, says set designer Kate Sutton-Johnson: "In a breakthrough moment I feel so much reward, but there's so much time that I spend when I don't know what that breakthrough is. That's really stressful. Huge musicals can be daunting. They are a puzzle, with lots of moving parts and pieces. I'll be sitting in my studio thinking I have no idea what the answer is, but I just know if I push at it long enough, if I just use the process that I know works, I know I will figure it out."

You shouldn't have the word "can't" in your vocabulary. You should always be in conversation with your limits.

—ARTISTIC DIRECTOR JACK REULER

. . . hierarchy, and a flexible hierarchy.

No theater project could function without a recognizable hierarchy, however ragtag. Directors rule. But while the director is at the rudder, many other people are in the boat rowing hard.

Playwright Kira Obolensky: "There are people in the theater who are very hierarchical and tend to believe that whatever they're seeing is the vision of a person. But I would argue that it's actually the vision of a lot of people. The vision is a collaboration of many people, and I recognize that."

Playwright and storyteller Kevin Kling describes a successful collaboration as being like "two molecules that have to come together, and the problem is you don't want to bump anyone's nucleus. When collaborations fall apart, I feel it's because people have interloped on other people's nucleus. I firmly believe the theater is not a democracy. It's a hierarchy in which

Set designer Kate Sutton-Johnson in her Northeast Minneapolis studio, working on half-inch scale model components for *Guys and Dolls.* (Photo by Amy Anderson)

everyone has their job. Of course actors will influence the direction, the designers will influence the direction, the play will influence the direction, but when push comes to shove, it's the one who stages the piece who's got the final say. That's the job a director has. Basically, in these situations, the playwright is the first one out of the picture—just kind of waving from the dock. You have to let something that might have only been in your head go."

. . . not making a great deal of money.
Few do.

You might belong in the theater if you . . .

. . . are skilled.
Skill is a must, both for individual satisfaction and fulfillment and for that of others. It's a meritocracy; everyone must be the best they can be at what they do.

. . . are resilient.
Rejection is an inevitable part of the work. Actors are rejected all the time in auditions. Everyone else's decisions are subject to rejection at any time. Each person has to bring their personal best, and then be willing to cut it and come up with another best. Resilience is a professional necessity for everyone.

"I always just say: rise above it, dear boy. Rise above it." And that does make me feel better.

—ACTOR RICARDO VAZQUEZ, QUOTING SIR TYRONE GUTHRIE,
    VIA ACTOR CHARLES KEATING

Actor and playwright Kevin Kling during a benefit at the Dakota Jazz Club. (Photo by Tom Sandelands)

. . . are brave.

Most of the work of the theater, past the solitary and imaginative stages, happens in public. In development and design meetings, in rehearsals, and in performances, the work of each member of the company is out there for everyone to see. They are being judged every minute. "Everyone has skin in the game," says artistic director Peter Rothstein, "and it is still an ego-based art form. Every aspect of the production is a reflection on the makers.

It's a reflection of the artistic director, of the play they chose, the director they chose. It's clearly a reflection of the actors' work, the designers' work. There's ego in the game."

. . . have a mordant sense of humor.

Battlefield humor; gallows humor—both are useful, because, metaphorically speaking, the project could die at any moment. Occasionally, a distinct urge to murder coworkers might be felt, also metaphorically speaking. That said, theater people say they laugh harder in theater work than anywhere else in their lives. Wit is the lingua franca. The stage manager who can use humor on a weary and rebellious company being asked to repeat the same scene for the ninth time while the fog machine is being adjusted—that person can prevent, or at least delay, meltdown.

And, as actor Sally Wingert says, laughing, "If somebody doesn't have a sense of humor, and I just mean the ability to laugh at your own stuff, then don't get into theater. Because, my gosh, it's going to be so sad!"

. . . are collegial, or at least collaborative.

Nothing in the theater happens alone. Everything accomplished depends to some extent on someone else.

. . . and also solitary.

Playwrights write for a long time, largely without knowing their work will be produced. They must, by definition, be alert to the existence of all sizes of ideas in the world, to recognize them and bring them to the page, with which they will sit, all alone, until it's done.

If designing is what you want to do, you need to be designing.
You shouldn't be doing a lot of other stuff.

—DESIGNER MARCUS DILLIARD

. . . have strong opinions, and the ability to swallow them.

No milquetoasts, please. It's best to have an opinion, and then be prepared to toss it aside and carry out someone else's opinion. Says Kira Obolensky, "I understand when things really do have to be cut. I don't think things are precious. I feel that a play I'm writing is just so malleable; I love that about it."

This mindset is good for playwrights in process; it's also critical for designers, actors, and everyone else. Lighting designer Marcus Dilliard reflects, "If you're worth anything as a lighting designer, you're going to find fault with every other lighting design that's out there. You have to have strong opinions about it, or you should not be a designer."

. . . are affable, or at least not confrontational.

Sound designer C. Andrew Mayer observes, "If there's a choice between people whose work is more or less comparable, but one of them is much more pleasant to be around in two weeks of fourteen-hour days, then you're going to opt for the pleasant one. I'm an American and a Minnesotan, so I'm eternally optimistic and cheerful and all that. Show up on time with a smile. That's what I've found."

. . . have both ego and humility.

Sally Wingert respects this balance: "I feel that a theater artist has this odd double-edged sword. You have to have enough ego to feel that you have every right to have people spend money to watch you do something. By the same token, you need to walk humbly in your profession, because as soon as you think you are the queen, within moments someone is going to let you know you aren't. Nobody goes alone. Nobody's a superstar. You have the pleasure of being an artist in a community."

On one day each year, many members of the fast-moving Twin Cities theater community take a brief pause to gather together. On this day they applaud each other at the Ivey Awards, at which theater folk look, behave, and shriek like a real community. In 2014, the Iveys, established to celebrate and increase awareness for professional theater in the Twin Cities, marked its tenth anniversary. In New York, the Tonys, of course. In Chicago, the

Jeffs. In London, the Oliviers. But in the Twin Cities people celebrate at the Iveys, dressed up and ready to party. It's a busy day for hair and makeup people.

All the requisite characters attend the ceremony: the impossibly beautiful of both genders and all sexual identities and orientations; the legendary (read "hoary") old-timers; funders and corporate folk mingling with the creatives; the young and the extremely young, who shriek at nearly everything they see, causing the hoary ones to flinch slightly in their seats. Hot music comes from a full orchestra in the pit, led by one of the Twin Cities' storied music directors. The house is so full that will-call spills over from the box office windows to tables in the lobby, where beleaguered box office workers struggle with seat assignments and requests; theater people definitely know where they want to sit.

Energy is high, the patter is bright, the evening brisk and entertaining, and the awards are duly awarded. Since the results are a closely held secret, some recipients must make their way from the high balcony all the way down to the stage, while waiting presenters smile continuously and shade their eyes toward the aisles.

After the show, the entire crowd spills out onto Hennepin Avenue, the street where the old burlesque houses once stood, to rustle and jumble and look at each other, lauding the winners carrying their awards, happily deafened by street drummers, downlit under the marquee lights, and stalking off to the After Party across the street. Hipster glasses. Vintage dresses. Beautiful headwear. Improbable shoes. Enthusiasm and energy and mutual admiration. And all on a Monday, so anyone can be there. Set designer Kate Sutton-Johnson says, "I always say I've met the best people I know and the worst people I know—all in the theater. I can hardly believe they even walk on this planet because I think they're so amazing." Many of the amazing can be seen at the Iveys.

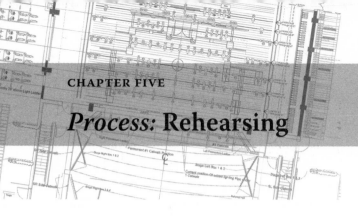

CHAPTER FIVE

Process: Rehearsing

There is nothing like the first rehearsal for a new production, for possibility, audacity, and sheer nerves. For actors, this is the moment at the top of the roller coaster. Staff have already been on board for some time, but until the director and designers and producers and marketers hear the play spoken aloud by the performers who will bring *Chosen Play* to life, the rest of the company is only imagining an artwork without its most important component. This is also the day when the artistic staff begin the process of giving the artwork over to the inevitable growth and twisting of the actors who now hold it in their hands. This is the day when all becomes discernible.

Some theaters have dedicated rehearsal rooms, and some rent space, which might be in church basements or old warehouses. Conditions can vary from the beautiful to the tolerable to the strictly utilitarian, but there are still customs associated with first readings. Stage managers have generally had a week or so of preparation and organization before actors arrive. Scripts for *Chosen Play* were distributed to the cast, tables were arranged in a circle with the correct number of chairs for participants, a separate director's table was set up, and chairs were placed off to the side for key listeners. Each place at the table has been supplied with a notepad and pencil, or at least room for an iPad. There are copies of scene breakdowns, contact sheets, and cast lists. A floor plan has been posted on a wall, and the stage shape has been measured and marked out on the floor. Shortly before the reading begins, pitchers of water, and perhaps a side table with bagels and cream cheese, are set up to fortify the group. As Hamlet says, "the readiness is all."

If the show is carrying a dramaturge, stacks of research material on

Chosen Play, its period, or its cultural references might also be in the rehearsal room. Often, costume sketches, or renderings, are posted; and a scale model of the scenery, perhaps intricate and painted, sits on a nearby table. These last two items, providing the first glimpse of the physical world of the play, attract much interest from everyone.

Good humor abounds on first rehearsal days, as people start to come in, singly and in groups. Actor bags, the industry equivalent of gym bags, appear by all the chairs, stuffed with clothes and shoes, water bottles, and reference texts. Many of the theater staff come to meet and welcome the company. The room fills with chatter: you've lost weight; you've gained weight; you've had a baby; I saw your show; I've been out of town. And there is business to conduct: forms to fill out, introductions to be made.

Coming to order, the director often talks for a time about her approach

Peter Brosius talks through the set design with stage manager Sam Houkom for *The Scarecrow and His Servant* at the first rehearsal day's "Meet and Greet" at the Children's Theatre Company. (Photo by Kaitlin Randolph)

to the play; each designer describes his work—the clothes, the scenery, the lights, the music. Each listener adds this imaginary landscape to his or her own visualization of the work to come, and a common vision starts to form. On the prereading break, actors cluster around the model and the renderings, fleshing out their impressions.

When people return to their places and open their scripts, a hush falls over the room. People settle in their chairs or sit forward. In the moment before the first words of the play are spoken, all pores are open and receptive. Here comes the first reading, and here come the rehearsals.

Six Weeks (or Less) Before Opening Night: Rehearsing

✓ Writing the Play   ✓ Finding the Audience
✓ The Decision to Produce   ✓ Rehearsing
✓ Assembling the Team   Technical and Dress Rehearsals
✓ Casting the Show   Opening Night

Actors arrive relatively late in the overall process but bring life with them into rehearsals—their own lives, certainly, plus their talent and dedication and energy; they also bring the life of *Chosen Play*. Plays are not meant to be read on the page. They are written to be spoken. Actors prepare to inhabit a role, not just to "play" it. In many cases, and for many actors, that means a research cycle of their own.

When actor Ricardo Vazquez was preparing for *Oedipus El Rey* for Teatro del Pueblo and Pangea World Theater, he had plenty of research to do. The show transports the Sophocles tragedy to South Central Los Angeles. Vazquez notes, "I had about three or four months to really prepare and work on this character, and I really knew that I had to fully commit myself to this, a very different life than mine. I specified where he was incarcerated, an actual place in California."

To prepare for his role as Oedipus, Vazquez contacted the prison to find out what equipment was in the gym. He then based his personal workout routine on using only the equipment that was available to the inmates. Three months later, he had put on about thirty pounds of muscle. He recalls,

Ricardo Vazquez as the title character in *Oedipus El Rey*, in a production for Teatro del Pueblo and Pangea World Theater. Directed by Dipankar Mukherjee. (Photo by Marc Norberg)

"It was like body armor on him [the character], and you're going to carry that energy into the room and into the space. I got rid of all my curly hair, and had all these designs put in my hair. And when we got back in the room and the text, this guy was just there."

Of portraying Oedipus El Rey, Vazquez says, "It can only be made of smoke and mirrors, because you haven't lived his life. You haven't gone through the penitentiary. But in those moments, those lines, and those scenes, I definitely had." When Vazquez began rehearsing the play, he brought his research, his muscle, and his altered hair into the room with him from the very first day.

First readings are revelatory. They offer the first glimpse at the shape of the envisioned artwork; everyone hears the same speech from the director. Chanhassen Dinner Theatres artistic director Michael Brindisi puts a lot of time into preparing. He uses the time to "rally everyone into a state of like-mindedness, while I set the stage for the important work we're about to do. I use art, music, electronic media, and always personal stories to support the thoughts and feelings I want to share about the play. My goal is always to unify the group and set the tone."

For the director and the designers, this is their first chance to get a look at the realities upon which they've been basing their plans and designs. For the theater administrators, particularly the marketing and promotions staff, it's the first moment when they get a clear sense of what they'll be

Artistic director Michael Brindisi addresses the company on first rehearsal day for *Hello, Dolly!* at Chanhassen Dinner Theatres. (Photo courtesy of Chanhassen Dinner Theatres)

presenting to their audience. For the actors, this is the first time they hear each other in their characters, and sometimes the first time they meet. There she is: your love interest, your best pal, the one you'll murder in the second act.

"I love that first reading," says actor T. Mychael Rambo. "I love to hear the voices of my fellow cast members breathing life into the page for the first time. It's the most honest of the whole process, because it's laden with so many rocky moments. We stumble over words or we fumble and miss the intention of a phrase. Sitting around the table we discover things that we didn't even plan on."

The first reading also marks one of the very rare occasions when all the interested parties are in the room together. After this, the activity necessary to making the play will disperse to the rehearsal rooms, the shops, the stage house, and, most importantly, the little furnaces of each mind

Director Richard Cook with actor Steve Lee Johnson, in rehearsal for *Red*, a play about artist Mark Rothko, taken in the scene shop at the University of Minnesota. Under discussion: how to paint convincingly on stage. (Photo by Petronella J. Ytsma)

and talent involved in the play's making. Moments of recognizable common intention, when everyone is looking at the work at the same time and from the same direction, are rare and become even rarer as the pace and pressures increase. There's a lot of work to do before run-throughs, when the whole play can be seen.

Rehearsal schedules vary tremendously in their details from theater to theater, but most are effectively more than full time. In large houses with union relationships, the hours are set by contract. Tuesday through Sunday is a common workweek; a day off on Monday is nearly universal. That is a

To the people who want to perform, please don't think of this as a profession, unless it's the only thing you can do. Unless you are so passionate, so obsessed, so in love and in need of that work that it's what you must do. Otherwise, it's too hard.

—ARTISTIC DIRECTOR RICHARD COOK

six-day workweek. A single day off, or, as the joke sometimes goes, one day off in a row. The rehearsal workdays, if they are controlled by agreements with the actors' union, are referred to as seven out of nine, or eight out of ten; that is, seven hours out of a nine-hour span, or eight hours out of a ten-hour span. Noon to five o'clock, two-hour dinner break, and then seven to ten would fall under the latter. Rehearsals generally start in the afternoon, to allow actors time in the mornings, which might be used for living the rest of their lives or, well, a part-time job.

The span of the rehearsal day is usually posted for the entire rehearsal period, so that the company can make plans. The setting of the daily rehearsal schedule is the work of the stage manager, whose own customary workday often runs to twelve hours. An easy-to-implement schedule calls for every actor to be present for every hour of rehearsal. A more humane schedule is broken out by scene and actor, thereby releasing actors when they are not actually needed on stage, but this is much more time consuming to plan, especially on a daily basis. When actors are not in the primary rehearsal, they may still need to be in the theater for costume fittings, for separate scene rehearsals, or for doing fight choreography or musical training or accent work. They might be asked to talk to journalists, a desirable use of time from the standpoint of the producer. *Chosen Play* is going to need an audience, and soon. And, of course, they are memorizing lines. Sooner or later, they must put down the scripts and go off book.

Actor Bradley Greenwald knows the freelance life well. He explains, "You don't know what your schedule is until the evening before that day. You have a rehearsal block, but you don't know if you'll be called the whole day, or two hours in the morning; in that sense, you're on call day after day after day. No day is the same. You don't even know what that day is going to be until you go to bed the evening before it."

Some actors, very lucky and hardworking ones, are in rehearsal and performance for a substantial number of weeks in every year. A great majority, many of whom are no less hardworking and skilled, work a decidedly unsubstantial number of weeks spread out over that same year. Rehearsal periods, depending on the show, can last anywhere from a few weeks to a few months. Regardless of the length of the rehearsal and performance

Jeremy Cohen, producing artistic director of the Playwrights' Center, in rehearsal for *Brahman/I*, with playwright Aditi Kapil. (Photo by Heidi Bohnenkamp)

phase, actors and show folk customarily work on a schedule that is nearly completely opposite to the rest of the world.

In a rehearsal-only schedule, for example, actors can be called for six long days a week in an afternoon-and-evening framework. In a performance-only schedule for an eight-show week, an industry standard involves working Tuesday through Sunday nights, plus two matinees. When there's no matinee, there are afternoon rehearsals. For actors performing at one theater and rehearsing at a different one, the hours can be even more extended.

A working actor might have all of Monday off, working every other night in the week, plus two afternoons. Actors are often unavailable for going out with friends or families, or for giving dinner parties, or for attending weddings. If they are partnered with someone not in the business, they are a professional couple on opposite work schedules. Their only time together, effectively, may be Monday nights, plus Saturday and Sunday mornings. During the week, they sleep together, but they don't intersect much otherwise. Regardless of how the day has gone or what tomorrow may bring, a working actor must rise to the peak of her powers for every show. Actors go on; that is the work and that is the profession.

By the end of the rehearsal period, days and weeks have been spent in the intensity of the rehearsal room, where the work is made. For artistic director Michelle Hensley, the rehearsal room is a joy—the place where she gets to work with people who are imaginative and generous and funny. "Most of the time," she says, "my job is to go into this room and laugh with people and have people make me laugh. So few people have that kind of job in this world. I make sure that the people who come to that room are people who bring all the best humanity has to offer into that space. I need

Playwright Kira Obolensky (*left*) and director Michelle Hensley, watching rehearsal for Obolensky's *Forget Me Not When Far Away* at the Playwrights' Center. (Photo by Heidi Bohnenkamp)

to create a space where everyone in the room feels safe, where they feel like they can be playful, they can be silly, they can make fools of themselves, they can be generous, and they can be kind. Artists must be allowed to be themselves, and make the kind of deep, committed, imaginative choices that I know they're capable of."

Actor and director Randy Reyes says that he'd be happy to "be in rehearsal forever. It's the process of discovery: learning and company building and the exchange of stories. We get to analyze humanity and unpack humanity. No one can bother us and we can fail freely as we try to accomplish something that's impossible; it's an impossible task to tell the story 'right.' So it's the pursuit of telling it the best that you can."

The lines of *Chosen Play* are memorized and linked to the physical action. The show is "blocked," meaning that each movement on the stage is planned and set. Rehearsal scenery stands in for the real thing that will come. Rehearsal props, intended to be as close as possible to the pieces now being sought and bought and built, are handled. Racks of rehearsal clothes, usually scruffy, stand in the corners—capes, long skirts and petticoats, hats, bodices, tailcoats, sword belts. These tools all contribute to the actors' work. As they rehearse, the stage—its shape taped out to the inch on the floor of the rehearsal room—is regularly filled with sound and fury.

All theater is a work of collective imagination and suspension of disbelief, but the rehearsal period makes special demands. It requires a collective agreement that masking tape on a floor represents the edge of a stage, and if you step across it you will fall off. A stage manager calling out "Bang!" means a gunshot. You can die gracefully on what will at some point be a Victorian fainting couch, but at the moment it's a threadbare sofa of inde-

For young actors: You should be observers in the rehearsal room.
Put your phones down and start watching what's going on.

—ACTOR SALLY WINGERT

terminate period and shaky construction. On a folding chair at the edge of your vision, while you are working on your important monologue, one of your colleagues is unwrapping and then devouring his lunch.

There's an old joke, perhaps apocryphal, about an actor, of cartoonishly haughty and mannered demeanor, who stands in a rehearsal room staring at a masking tape X in the middle of the floor. He queries the stage manager: "Remind me, please. Is this the tree or the rose bush?" The stage manager replies, "It's a fountain." The actor cries out in real dismay, "Oh, no! But that changes everything!"

Concentration is required. Actor Ricardo Vazquez says, "There's no difference between rehearsing and performing to me. Every rehearsal is a hundred percent commitment to the character you're working on. There are days when you understand more about the character, and days when you understand less, but in my body, I always have to be committed as though there were twelve hundred people watching this moment."

Rehearsal is an ongoing act of will and imagination, in which the actor must visualize and occupy a world that does not yet exist, making it manifest in his every word and action and calling it up for his own eye, so that later the audience will be able to see it, too. Bradley Greenwald reveals, "I don't think most audience members are aware of how many choices were made to get to the choice they're seeing in performance." He uses the example of how you close a door in character. "Perhaps in rehearsal you just came in and left the door open, and started the scene. Then something wasn't right about that. So then you come in and you casually shut the door. That didn't seem to feed the scene very well, so you come in and slam the door. Well, that was the wrong choice because it starts the scene with a bang, and it needs to start with a whisper."

"The audience doesn't know of the whole week you spent failing at shutting that door over and over again," says Greenwald. "The director didn't know what it should be like and you didn't know, and other colleagues didn't know, and you've tried all these different ways of closing that door, and none of them seem to work."

"Then, finally, in tech [technical rehearsal]," Greenwald continues, "you were tired and you weren't even doing the scene. You just came in the door and you stopped and grabbed the doorknob, and you very slowly shut it until it clicked. Suddenly, a light bulb goes up and you have a discovery. That's the way you should enter the scene."

In a perfect world, or even a nearly perfect world, by the end of the rehearsal period, the shape of *Chosen Play* has developed to the director's intention. The company has found its rhythm and pace and is approaching the most effective method for telling the story to the yet-imaginary audience. A thousand details have been considered, transmitted to the appropriate person, decided on, and acted upon. Stage managers have filled reams of notebooks—or megabytes of files and emails—with notes. ("Pouf will need padding for actor collapse." "Sheep have been cut per director." "Will she be able to run in her skirt and bustle?" "Fog will need to last two minutes and thirty seconds.") The play has been run without stopping—more than once—so that lighting and sound designers can plan their work, soon to be added to the mix, and so the company can find its overall rhythm with the story.

Once actors begin doing run-throughs of *Chosen Play*, the ownership of the rehearsals can broaden. Actor H. Adam Harris observes, "First [the play] belonged to us as individuals, but when we start to do runs, then it belongs to the ensemble again. All of us are now responsible for keeping this ball in the air and holding it. The final run before tech is incredible."

Next step: everything stops. Pack up those actor bags and move into the dressing rooms. Abandon the rehearsal room; the show is taking the stage.

Two Weeks (or So) Before Opening:
Technical and Dress Rehearsals

- ✓ *Writing the Play*
- ✓ *The Decision to Produce*
- ✓ *Assembling the Team*
- ✓ *Casting the Show*
- ✓ *Finding the Audience*
- ✓ *Rehearsing*
- ✓ *Technical and Dress Rehearsals*
-   *Opening Night*

During the technical and then the dress rehearsal phase, the pace increases and intensifies. All the missing elements, the ones that have been imagined, will now be added. The technicians have been hanging lights, focusing them on particular areas of the stage, adding color to lights, hooking it all up, and testing it. Likewise, the sound folks have been setting up their tools: speakers and wire, computers and sound files. The costumes have been racked and moved into the dressing rooms. The worktables for the stage manager, for lighting, and for sound are in the house. Prop tables are in the wings. Special effects have been hooked up and tested—fog, trapdoors, rigging. Headset systems are ready so that all the crew folk can be connected. The house sound system is turned on so that actors waiting offstage can hear the progress of the play. The stage manager has tested what is often called the "God mic," the microphone that will be used to speak to everyone, everywhere. On stage or off, in the house or the dressing rooms, everyone will receive calls and break notices.

Lighting designer Marcus Dilliard *(left)* with director Peter Rothstein at the lighting table during technical rehearsals for *M. Butterfly* at the Guthrie. (Photo by Michal Daniel)

In tech rehearsals, everything that was visualized must become real. All possibilities for brilliant fulfillment of the ideas are in the room. At the same time, all possibilities stand in jeopardy.

In order to appreciate technical rehearsals, lighting designer Marcus Dilliard says, "You have to love chaos. My career is all about tech rehearsals, the part of the process that directors and performers hate. You have to love tech, because you're part of a very small team—sometimes just you and the stage manager—who are bringing order out of chaos." If you don't like doing that, Dilliard continues, "you have no business being a lighting designer or a stage manager. You should find something else to do. The lighting table is sort of the rock, the island in the middle of the tempest, the way the stage management table should be. Those are the two things that directors will hold onto during tech."

Moving into the theater for tech rehearsals can trigger some bumps in the road to opening. Rehearsal momentum can be lost as the company encounters the physical world of *Chosen Play*: real (or stage-real) walls and windows and doors and stairs; real costumes, with bustiers and fly-front trousers and period-looking shoes. The rough crockery and mismatched wine glasses used in rehearsal are replaced with something beautiful but fragile that requires special handling. Balcony scenes now have a real balcony.

In this tech phase, the enclosing walls, the familiarity, and the intimacy of the rehearsal room are gone. The actors' voices sound different on the performance stage. The director and creative team are now watching from every corner of the house and from all the extreme sightlines. Can the character be seen? Can she be heard? Does that tree or bush or fountain match what had been visualized? Can the character climb the tree, hide behind the bush, or splash in the fountain, as the action requires? Performances have to be lifted up and made the right size to reach every seat in the house.

Actor Anna Sundberg loves the tech phase, which, she says, feels like Christmas: "It's like a big gift. Huge decisions are made and you've just got to lock it down. You could have been fiddling with a lot of different takes on something. But, knife coming down. All right, this is what we're doing. You've just got to get things done."

The time before the audience fills the seats is full of preparation and anticipation on stage and backstage. Here, lighting designer Jesse Cogswell focuses a light on stage at the Ordway. (Photo by Michal Daniel)

During technical rehearsals, each design team occupies an outpost in the empty theater—a lighting table with a few ranks of computers and iPads, with desk lights hunched over everything to preserve night vision for the designers; another table with a sound board, computers, and good headsets. The costume shop claims an area, with no tables but with a good view of the stage and with reasonably convenient access for actors to pop offstage and ask questions. The stage manager, who now rules supreme, coordinates and commands from a stage management table. Everything is connected by headset and cable, taped down in the aisles and seat rows. The director, dramaturge, and various assistants are camped out, usually in the very best seats and centrally located for ease in talking to everyone else. Technicians scoot through the dark. Occasional administrators and staff people pop into the back of the house for a look at *Chosen Play* before rushing back to sell tickets or manage opening-night events.

Still, from the stage, particularly under work lights, the actors can see rank upon rank of empty seats. Here, shortly, is where the last most crucial component of the theater will be added to the equation.

CHAPTER SIX

The Twin Cities: Why the Theater Community Is Strong

Why, 'tis a happy thing to be the father unto many sons.
—William Shakespeare, *Henry VI, Part III*

The theater community of today—large, mobile, inventive—springs from a long line of theater people, of all types, stretching back decades and longer. Many young practitioners do not tend to think of their predecessors at all. More mature theater people gain perspective by necessity, as their own earlier roles and shows fall back into the past. Theater is brutally brief, existing only in memory once the curtain falls, but it is constructed of individual efforts, and over time, it is the individuals who build the future as they themselves recede into the past. People have come before, they have worked just as hard, they have had their triumphs and tragedies, and in historical terms, we are building new rooms in a house they constructed.

Frank M. Whiting, the "Doc" Whiting who wrote the first invitation letter to Tyrone Guthrie about founding a theater in Minneapolis, wrote a fascinating book in 1988 called *Minnesota Theatre: From Old Fort Snelling to the Guthrie*. In it, Whiting traces a complex development web that, he says, started in 1821 with bored soldiers at Fort Snelling making their own entertainment by acting out melodramas of the time. Traveling road companies, stock companies, and eventually resident companies found a home in the Twin Cities, even if for just a few shows or a few seasons. In 1883, two separate Grand Opera Houses were being constructed, one in each city. In 1897, the Drama Club at the University of Minnesota attempted the classics with eighteenth-century playwright Richard Brinsley Sheridan's *The Rivals* and Shakespeare's *Twelfth Night*.

Ethnic theaters, Whiting says, formed a continuous thread of connection in their own communities; he writes about a strong Yiddish theater, Scandinavian performers, and an amateur German-language theater system which he describes as having a "long and abundant history." By 1930, Minnesota was home to the oldest and most successful stock company in the nation. When that company disbanded three years later, its owner and manager was elected mayor of Minneapolis. He served just one term in office; apparently he had a "sunny disposition" but no municipal experience. Road companies visited throughout the 1940s and 1950s, and strong local companies such as Don Stolz's Old Log Theatre (founded in 1940) and Dudley Riggs's Brave New Workshop (1958) kept the dramatic flame alive. Both of these professional companies are still performing, as is the Theatre in the Round Players, a community theater that began in 1953 and is now located on the West Bank of Minneapolis.

At the University of Minnesota, the University Theatre presented both on campus and off, working in cooperation with the Minneapolis Symphony and with the university's language departments for productions of French, German, and Spanish plays in their original languages. Leadership of the American Educational Theatre Association was concentrated on the university campus in the mid-fifties. In 1958, an energetic group of professors formed an alliance with the Minnesota Centennial Commission to celebrate the state's milestone birthday. The medium they chose: a refurbished riverboat, on which theater students would perform melodramas while floating on the Mississippi River. The descendant of that university showboat still operates today.

About the same time, University of Minnesota professor Arthur Ballet, a spellbinding lecturer, began teaching a class called Introduction to the Theater. It became legendary for its popularity and enrollment, reportedly limited only by the size of the largest available hall in which it could be held. For at least seventeen years, the numbers grew, to as many as 2,700 students per year by the 1970s. Ballet's passion for the theater fostered enthusiasm in his students and served to train a younger generation of theater audience members, eventually totaling in the tens of thousands. As retired professor C. Lance Brockman recalls, "What was apparent to me was that the Guthrie, the Children's Theatre Company, Penumbra, they all put the profound interest in theater in this community to the fact that Arthur Ballet was committed to creating audiences."

By 1963, the Twin Cities had a fine-art museum, a well-respected symphony, and good competing newspapers. Professional sports had arrived in 1961 with both the Minnesota Twins baseball team and a professional football expansion team, the Vikings. All of these amenities were touted as solid civic indicators during the sales pitch that brought the Guthrie Theater to Minneapolis in 1963. The Guthrie's arrival changed everything.

Tyrone Guthrie, probably the best-known English-speaking theater director in the world at the time, had begun to tire of the vagaries and constrictions of New York and Broadway by the mid-1950s. In 1953, in Ontario, Canada, Guthrie and his colleagues had opened the Stratford Festival, with its remarkable thrust-shaped stage and an aesthetic that included contemporary interpretations of the great works of the classical theater canon.

His work in North America led Guthrie and several colleagues to dream of a classical repertory company that would be founded far from the constraints of the commercial theater scene in New York City. On September 30, 1959, through a nationally published theater column in the *New York Times*, Guthrie invited interested cities to contact him. In Minnesota, Dr. Frank Whiting, then the head of the theater department at the University of Minnesota, wrote a letter inviting Guthrie and his colleagues to consider Minneapolis. A committee of civic leaders, many of them young and influential, went to work to attract the famous director to the city, touting its advantages, competing with delegations from Milwaukee, Detroit, and other cities. The committee even flew to New York for a day, unheard of at the time, for a lunch meeting at the Century Club.

The committee prevailed. In 1963, the brand-new Guthrie Theater opened with a production of *Hamlet* in a contemporary setting, complete with tuxedos and flashlights. The founding was famously described, then and now, as "planting an oak tree." Guthrie and his Twin Cities collaborators brought superb actors, the rigor of a rolling repertory system, and a sparkling new theater building to Minneapolis. The Twin Cities and the local theater profession would never be the same.

The wild civic excitement surrounding the opening of the Guthrie Theater in 1963 can scarcely be overstated. Hundreds of Minnesotans participated in the board and community leadership work involved in building and opening the physical theater, and an enormous corps of volunteers fanned out through the Twin Cities, simultaneously selling enthusiasm and tickets. During the fundraising period, the tall and elegant Tyrone Guthrie, with his upper-class British accent, was knighted by Queen Elizabeth II, which, we can assume, mightily impressed the citizenry of Minnesota. Stories about the theater opening were carried in almost every daily newspaper in the United States and Canada. The event, according to *Newsweek* magazine, attracted out-of-town drama critics "as thick as the smelt running the northern streams." One remark from the *New York Times* seems particularly prescient: "There is here something of the mood of a Stockholm or an Oslo . . . a mixture of sophistication and brawny love of the outdoors in the state of 10,000 lakes. . . . Affluence, a high educational level and civic leadership, combined with the spirit of a small town in the midst of a metropolis, have set the stage for Sir Tyrone Guthrie's triumphant entrance."

In the first few years, the Guthrie operated as a summer festival, following their *Hamlet* with remarkable productions of *The Cherry Orchard*, *The Caucasian Chalk Circle*, and *The House of Atreus*. The season became a little longer, and then longer again, still opening in June but running into the fall. There were perilous times—even the oak tree was not immune to the theatrical imperative of filling seats and staying solvent—but Minnesota had adopted the idea of its own classical theater and made it a signature part of its civic identity.

Working teams form around projects and, sometimes, continue to work together thereafter. Communities form around theaters as much as theaters form around communities. Tyrone Guthrie came, he brought colleagues, and over successive seasons he attracted others to the company. Those colleagues became members of the community, living in neighborhoods, shopping in grocery stores, walking around lakes. Among the most famous were the wizardly designer Tanya Moiseiwitsch and leading actors of the day, such as George Grizzard, Hume Cronyn, Jessica Tandy. For decades, some would return to do an occasional show—actors Ken Ruta, Peter Michael Goetz, and Helen Carey—and some would make their permanent homes here—costume shop cofounder Annette Garceau and actor James Lawless.

Communities feed each other; like attracts like. In the rich cross-pollination that was happening in Twin Cities theater, growth was rapid. Looking back, actor Bradley Greenwald reflects, "We were very lucky that we didn't end up with the Guthrie and maybe [a] half dozen other Guthrie wannabes, theaters who were doing the same aesthetic on a smaller scale. What happened was you got all these different troupes and companies and theaters popping up, creating with their own discipline and their own aesthetic."

The Moppet Players, predecessor to the Children's Theatre Company, moved into the Minneapolis Institute of Arts in 1965. Chanhassen Dinner Theatres were founded in 1968. The Cricket Theatre opened in 1968 and ran for twenty-six years. Park Square Theatre in St. Paul presented its first season in 1972; In the Heart of the Beast Puppet and Mask Theatre in 1973; the Illusion Theater in 1974; Mixed Blood Theatre in 1976; Penumbra Theatre in 1977; Theatre de la Jeune Lune and the History Theatre, both in 1978; Red Eye Collaboration in 1983; and the Jungle Theater in 1991.

Even the theaters that are no longer active—among them the Palace Theatre, At the Foot of the Mountain, Actors Theatre of St. Paul, Cricket Theatre, Eye of the Storm, and, perhaps most notably, Theatre de la Jeune Lune—were part of the complex web of effort and ambition that people make when a community is forming, then boiling and spilling over. Today's community stands on the shoulders of these theaters, and many artists from these companies went on to other theaters and other work in the Twin Cities.

Playwright Barbara Field remembers 1971 as a particularly fertile year, the same year that new artistic director Michael Langham regenerated an imperiled Guthrie Theater and ushered in a set of seasons some still remember as a golden age at that theater. Field notes that artistic fertility is not confined by discipline: "In one year, like spontaneous generation, four or five organizations came into existence: the Playwrights' Center, Film in the Cities, the Composer's Forum, the Loft Literary Center, and a dance aggregate that I think was called the Minnesota Dance Alliance. It happened because the community, or at least the funding community, was hungry for something more than a big theater. They funded these organizations that didn't produce. All they did was develop."

The Playwrights' Center is now one of the largest organizations of its kind in the country, and arguably one of the keys to the vitality of the Twin Cities theater community. It began on a very small scale, and once again, a class at the University of Minnesota is an important element of the story. Field, a founding member, recalls, "A small handful of playwrights from Charles Nolte's playwriting class got together in the early seventies and thought, 'Well, how can we get our plays produced? We need to be unified in some way to form leverage to get them seen and heard.' In the beginning, it wasn't any more than just wanting to have people hear our work. Every Saturday night, the designated playwright would buy a case of beer."

Field continues, "We started at 10:30 or 11 after other shows had come down so we could have actors, and people would stumble in and we could have an audience. It only occurred to us after a year or two, after we got a couple of productions, that we were missing something important. 'How can we make the plays better?' We can just sit here for a very long time, but we need some dramaturgical input. At that point the foundations came aboard, and that's how it began."

Chronology becomes elusive when considering the growth of something that might resemble various streams of water combining into a deep pool. One steady flow came from philanthropic institutions that provided a strong underpinning, particularly as societal expectations shifted away from an assumption that theater should pay for itself and toward a recognition that the value of arts activities warrants a measure of public and private support.

Teresa Eyring is the executive director of New York's Theatre Communications Group, an organization founded in 1961 to promote American theater. Eyring came through both the Guthrie and the Children's Theatre Company as a manager before moving to the national perch. Of theater in the Twin Cities she says, "In the sixties and seventies, when the theater movement was really taking off in this country, there was a very strong base of support. It was a combination of the resources that were generated through some of the major corporations and businesses in the Twin Cities, the philanthropic inclination of those companies and the families that founded them. These were people who really thought it was important. They came together with others who had financial resources and a passion about making the community as strong as it could be from a cultural perspective." Eyring also cites a unified sense of civic responsibility in the Twin Cities: "There's a sense of people really caring about the well-being of the community and giving something of themselves to ensure that is realized."

Teresa Eyring, executive director of Theatre Communications Group, welcomes theater leaders to a forum on governance, cash, and culture in New York. (Photo by Isaiah Tanenbaum)

Leaders in the theater community are most admiring, and most appreciative, of the philanthropic climate in the Twin Cities. Mixed Blood artistic director Jack Reuler reflects, "There's a saying that when fundraisers die and go to heaven, they go to Minneapolis. I think that philanthropy is actually born out of altruism, born out of belief in community. People in the philanthropic community are linking human services and the cultural climate. It's the major corporations, it's the family foundations, and the handing over of generational fortunes will only allow philanthropy to grow." Jeremy Cohen of the Playwrights' Center puts it another way. "For theater artists in particular, there is a really vibrant audience base here and a very highly intelligent philanthropic community. That perfect story allows a powerfully deep level of support."

Philanthropic dollars not only support arts institutions but also make direct support of theater artists possible. Playwrights' Center, for example, also supports the cluster of theater artists—actors, directors—who are necessary to the process of new play development. "If you think of artists as the thinkers of your society," says actor and playwright Aditi Kapil, "and if you look to our artists to be generating the work that will be most relevant in this moment, you want them fully fueled. You want them fully engaged in the world around them."

For Kapil, the availability of arts funding was an important component in her decision to establish a career in the Twin Cities and, she says, why she never moved to New York. "It made it possible for me, as a person subsisting in the arts, to explore all the other facets of what I could be as an art maker and to become a theater artist who does all of these things. Why? Because I didn't have to be waiting tables and running from audition to audition to then get a role that paid me bus fare, which is the reality in New York."

Public funding for the arts in Minnesota is also strong. Eyring is particularly struck by an effort unique to this state: "I've not heard of any other state that passed anything like the Legacy Amendment, where fishing and hunting and wildlife and the arts are in the same funding pool."

Reuler calls the Legacy Amendment a "significant game changer that really speaks to the progressive nature of a few politicians. That was won two-to-one during the lowest time in the American economy in the last sixty years. That speaks not just about how Minnesotans want clean water but also how they value the arts. We are at a time when the arts are recognized as a catalyst for change, as a quality of life ingredient that is undeniable."

The Clean Water, Land, and Legacy Amendment to the Minnesota constitution was shepherded into law in 2008 by Minnesota state senator Richard Cohen, a longtime theater and arts supporter. Linked to the sales tax, the amendment allows Minnesotans to invest more than $1.2 billion in Arts and Cultural Heritage Fund projects and programs over the twenty-five-year life of the tax. "Outdoor recreational activity is a significant part of life in Minnesota," says Cohen, "but arts and cultural activity is equally significant. My thought was if we're going to take care of one, we should take care of both."

Cohen is proud of the Legacy Amendment. He says, "If you look nationally, the combination of general fund and Legacy dollars going to the arts in Minnesota is very close to the expenditures in New York; we're number two. And on a per capita basis, Minnesota is number one by far."

From Cohen's perspective "not only as an audience member, but [also] as a government figure in the Twin Cities," he asserts, "I think the significance of the theatrical arts community is one of the defining parts of Twin Cities life. Our cultural life doesn't exist in many other places."

Philanthropic contributions and public funding support the growth in a creative community and build a climate hospitable to creators. The evidence for both growth and hospitality is ample. Children's Theatre Company artistic director Peter Brosius cites the wide range of individuals who chose to start a theater in the Twin Cities, "from Tyrone [Guthrie] to Jack Reuler to Michelle [Hensley] to Bonnie [Morris] and Michael [Robins] to Lou [Bellamy]. You've got a whole group of people, and more and more and more, who were able to take an idiosyncratic vision of what theater can and should be, and succeed in making the work they wanted to make. The fact that this community allowed, supported, encouraged, nurtured that, sets a tone for others. So you have a Pangea and you have a Mu Performing Arts and Teatro del Pueblo, extraordinary companies that make [the] work they want to make, for the audience they want to serve, and the aesthetics they want to work in. It is a community filled with engaging and inspiring artists. It is a joy to be part of that vision and energy."

An additional measure of attaining critical mass for health and longevity in the theater community is what might be called a deep bench. The number of institutions and theater people is certainly important, but so is a stratified community consisting of different layers of experience and professionalism. A self-sustaining and growing theater community needs enough senior artists who are reasonably successful and reasonably willing to serve as guides and mentors, even just by example, to the ones coming up. It's also necessary to have a strong enough community of peers to provide an atmosphere that can ignite artists looking for collaborators and for alignment of vision.

Mobility also matters. Young artists need to see a way to move up. Sound designer C. Andrew Mayer tells a story: "When I started, there were three of us who kind of had the town carved up, like the godfather families. We each had our own gigs that we did, and occasionally we would throw stuff at each other that we couldn't do. It was quite stable for a while there. Then the new Guthrie opened, and the other two got full-time jobs and dropped out of the freelance market. And I started getting bigger gigs and more gigs. People start to burble up, you know. People step up when there's a space for them."

Joe Dowling spent twenty seasons as artistic director of the Guthrie Theater. His colleague for nineteen years, John Miller-Stephany, feels that one of Dowling's major legacies is the University of Minnesota/Guthrie Theater BFA Actor Training Program, which had graduated ten classes of classically trained actors by the time of Dowling's final season at the Guthrie in 2014–15. The program has helped to cultivate a steady supply of passionate and talented young actors who have helped to revitalize the local theater scene. Miller-Stephany observes, "Many BFA students come here to study from out of town and fall in love with the Twin Cities. A good many of them stay after graduating, at least for a couple of years. Quite a few BFA graduates have decided that they want to call the Twin Cities their permanent home, and that's been transformative of the local theater community." The BFA actors and alumni have been seen everywhere on Twin Cities stages, appearing in more than sixty-eight theaters and in six hundred roles since the program's inception.

Another active entry point for young actors is the Children's Theatre Company's Performing Apprentice program. "One of our great pleasures," CTC's Peter Brosius says, "is the number of Performing Apprentices we've brought here from out of town, who make this their home, and make the city a better city because they're wonderfully talented young actors." These programs provide top-flight training, enrich the talent pool, and offer wonderful actor-watching to observant audience members.

A supply of good young actors is important to the community, but the bench has to be deep in more than one way; theater workers are not interchangeable. If you produce musicals, you need sufficient numbers of actors who can also sing and dance—a skill set sometimes called "triple threats." Working in Chekhov and Shakespeare? Better be counting on a large community of character actors. Producing new work? Those young actors will be needed in quantity—much new work is written with young characters—and everyone must understand how to do a new-script reading. Comedies and light entertainment? Particular boldness and terrific timing may be required, and that's before even considering the general baselines of talent and availability.

The quantity of theaters and theater-support organizations provides one way to measure liveliness in a community. Artists meet, work together, and trade ideas at these places. Theater companies pay attention to what their colleagues across town are doing; artists pay attention to what their

The real goal is to be able to do this for a living. See as much theater as you can. Find out the kind of artist you want to be, and then find a way to be around the people who are doing that kind of work.

—ARTISTIC DIRECTOR AND ACTOR RANDY REYES

peers are doing. Although finding time against performance schedules can be difficult, most working theater people try to see other work, not only for friendship and collegiality but also for inspiration. Everyone in the theater community supplies grist for the mill.

Another sign of health is evident when word spreads not just inside but also outside the community about what should be seen. Sometimes the interest level and rigor of a production rise enough to attract other theater artists to the community to see it, to participate in it, and perhaps to stay.

During the 1980s, under the leadership of artistic directors Liviu Ciulei and then Garland Wright, the Guthrie Theater invited leading theater artists from around the world to come to Minnesota to work for one show or a series of shows. Their presence here, and sometimes the opportunity to work directly with them, exposed Minnesotans to what was happening in the profession elsewhere in the world. Theater artists and audiences here saw the designs of Radu and Miruna Boruzescu, the directing of Lucien Pintilie and Peter Sellars and JoAnn Akalaitis, the lighting of Jennifer Tipton, and the scenery of John Arnone, among others. Most of these artists came for a portion of a season, or a few shows, and went flying on, although actors and staff who came during that period sometimes looked around and stayed. Practitioners of theater in the Twin Cities were regulars in the Guthrie audience during this time, ingesting the aesthetics, adapting and carrying them forward in their own creative projects, deepening the work here and encouraging more cross-fertilization.

Peter Brosius is another example of an artist who settled in Minnesota because of the strong work being done here, particularly citing Theatre de la Jeune Lune, the seminal and celebrated company that won a regional Tony Award in 2005 and is still often mentioned by theater professionals as influential to their own work. "I was a fan from afar," Brosius recalls. "I'd been following them for years. The idea that I could be in the community where Dominique [Serrand] and Steve [Epp] and that whole team was making work that rigorous, that inventive, that brilliantly theatrical was a big motivator to come here." Serrand's nontraditional theater, which was founded to play half the year in Minneapolis and half the year in Paris, closed in 2008 after years of what *Playbill* magazine described as "visually-stunning, mind-stirring work—often movement-oriented, projection-kissed, and theatrically multi-disciplinary." Serrand is now, with Epp, co-artistic director of the Moving Company.

Director Peter Rothstein also cites the work of Theatre de la Jeune Lune, along with the opportunity to assist then–artistic director Garland Wright at the Guthrie, as reasons he chose to settle in the Twin Cities.

The larger a community grows, the more easily it can provide another critical ingredient for growth and survival: opportunities for work—work to be had, work to be taken, work to feed artists as they find their way to a reasonable balance in the notoriously underpaid arts. When there is work to be had, artists will arrive to do it.

This institutional depth in a community crosses artistic disciplines and contributes to general cultural richness and fertility. Teresa Eyring notes the presence of "more than one very high-quality institution in any given discipline" as part of what is unusual and special about the Twin Cities. "You have the Minnesota Orchestra and the St. Paul Chamber Orchestra. You have the Children's Theatre Company, the flagship, and you also have Stages Theatre Company. And the museums. Where you might expect one major institution in the discipline, there are multiples."

This broad landscape provides room for both variety and quantity. "The Twin Cities theater community is unusual in the sense that there has always been very strong differentiation in the community," says Eyring. "You don't

One of the core values of Mixed Blood is every decision we make has to be good for the organization, good for the community, however defined, and good for the field. If the answer to any of those three is no, then we don't do it.

—ARTISTIC DIRECTOR JACK REULER

see a lot of replication. In some cities, there might be five or ten theaters that are all kind of doing the same sort of work, competing for the same material, getting rights to the same plays. In the Twin Cities, it was always really delineated. The Guthrie and its mission are very different from the Children's Theatre Company mission, which is very different from Penumbra, which is very different from Mixed Blood or Illusion. Very distinct. And I think that made it more likely that people go to multiple theaters to see these different kinds of work."

Mixed Blood's Jack Reuler agrees that the variation in types of theaters is one of the great assets of the Twin Cities—and beyond simple differentiation, there is high quality. Reuler remarks, "I believe that the Twin Cities have the best of the best for every genre that there is in the world of theater. The Children's Theatre is the best children's theater in the country. The Guthrie is the flagship institutional theater. I think Penumbra is the definitive African American theater. I think Mu Performing Arts is the great Asian American theater in the country. I think Chanhassen is the best dinner theater in America. I think Mixed Blood is the best Mixed Blood there is."

"I named half a dozen," Reuler continues, "but I could name another thirty. And every one has carved out a mission that is distinct from everyone else, that allows audience members—who might not even know yet that they want to be audience members—to have a place to go. Everybody is working together, so what we have to offer is a broad spectrum of aesthetics, and what theater can do."

In addition to the theater creators, the theatergoers, too, must grow and reach critical mass; their size and quality are a crucial component to the health of the community. Eyring acknowledges the remarkable artists "who have challenged audiences and brought them along. The audience [in the Twin Cities] might be a little different, a little more knowledgeable about the variety in types of theater. I think of people there as being more socially engaged, more politically active. It's that engagement with and caring about community that also makes people go to the theater and relate to the work. For a lot of people there, it's part of life, it's part of expressing your citizenship."

That necessary growth in the audience can be attributed to several factors. The place of the educational communities as breeders of audiences cannot be discounted. Nor can the decades of active cultivation of student audiences, now a critical regimen for many midsized and larger theaters, and begun at the Guthrie in its very first seasons. For decades, bright school buses have delivered a torrent of students to performances. In its early years, the Guthrie's regional tours reached tens of thousands of audience members in their own towns. Developing familiarity with and a taste for the theater in the populace, and particularly in young people, had no small hand in developing the audiences of today.

Michelle Hensley, artistic director of Ten Thousand Things Theater, discovered Twin Cities audiences to be a good match for the work of her socially conscious theater, which she had founded in Los Angeles. She observes, "People really enjoy going to the theater in the Twin Cities. And that was not true in LA, which is very much a film and TV town. The whole genesis of my company actually was LA theater audiences who, well, they come from duty, obligation, they've got friends in the cast, they are casting directors or agents. They would really rather be someplace else."

Peter Rothstein, artistic director of Theater Latté Da, also praises Twin Cities audiences: "Because of the amount of theater that happens here, there is satisfaction from an audience about the event itself, and the way it's told, as much as the story. The *how* the story is told is so much a part of the theater. This community has been so influenced by revolutionary directors at the Guthrie, by the work of Theatre de la Jeune Lune, by a profound modern dance community, the storytelling techniques and theatrical vocabulary. The theatrical motivation is as much of the event as the story that a given play tells."

Rothstein continues, "I saw a very traditional *Romeo and Juliet* over the summer. I thought, 'Oh my gosh, this is so musty.' We just don't do musty in our city anymore, if we ever did. Our audience is interested in the telling, not just the tale being told."

Jeff Larson, executive director of the Minnesota Fringe Festival. (Photo by Craig VanDerSchaegen)

A portion of the Twin Cities audience aligns itself very strongly with the Minnesota Fringe Festival, a phenomenon that features many different disciplines, and which has an important place in the yearly cycle. The Fringe in 2014 sold more than 50,000 tickets to 169 independently produced shows over eleven summer days. In contrast to other fringe festivals across the country, the Minnesota festival is entirely uncurated, with shows chosen in a live, onstage lottery (think party) where ping-pong balls are pulled from a bingo cage. With almost 500 applicants in 2014, some professional and some not, the Minnesota Fringe is highly indicative of a widespread ambition to perform.

The audience at the Fringe Festival consists of both practitioners and enthusiasts. According to executive director Jeff Larson, "We have a lot of people who take off work and see fifty-five shows—that's the maximum you can see on our schedule. These people get more and more excited every year and they talk about it year round."

What is the place of the wild and wooly Fringe in the Twin Cities theater community? "We're growing the audience," Larson says. "We're a gateway drug. The tickets are inexpensive, it's easy, you can dress however you want. Theater is not intimidating; it's not something you should do to better yourself. It's just another form of entertainment. We're getting that idea into people's heads."

Larson says the Fringe also acts as an incubator for the Twin Cities theater community. Citing the companies Walking Shadow, Four Humors, Gremlin, and Transatlantic Love Affair, he notes that people who come together for Fringe projects often continue working together: "Companies find their audiences here. Both shows and companies get pulled out of the Fringe and remounted elsewhere. It's a lake where other theater companies are fishing."

One remarkable thread in the development of the Twin Cities theater community is the founding, survival, and prospering of culturally specific theaters in the largely white Upper Midwest. Rick Shiomi is the founder of Mu Performing Arts and traces the theater's beginnings to foundation support. Shiomi says that while the issues of diversity were being addressed in the artistic communities on the West Coast or in New York, little was happening in Minnesota, at first. "But we caught the wave of interest and diversity that started happening in the late eighties or early nineties in Minnesota," he recollects. "Foundations were interested in the company we were founding because we were going to provide something that didn't exist and was going to add to the diversity of this theater community. This community is quite supportive, in many ways, of artists who are trying to do something different, or trying to do something of interest, or whose work they think is good."

Mu's artistic director, Randy Reyes, feels the philanthropic community in the Twin Cities is committed to supporting diversity, as are theater audiences: "Three things have enabled us to grow: the philanthropic community embracing diversity, the Asian American community that's growing, and the theater community that supports theater work. Without adventurous theatergoers—one of the things I love about the Twin Cities—and funding from the philanthropic community, we would not have survived."

Penumbra Theatre founder Lou Bellamy sometimes jokes with his audience by saying, "Yes, we are one of the largest African American theaters in the country. And yes, we're in Minnesota!" He says he subscribes to Booker T. Washington's principle that you "cast down your bucket where you are." "I was in the Twin Cities," Bellamy notes, "that was my home and that was where I began doing theater."

When Penumbra was founded in 1976, says co–artistic director Sarah Bellamy, it was "specifically with the idea of revisiting the black theater canon and giving opportunities for black actors to work. They were not getting work on other stages and when they were, it was quite limited and often stereotypical." Penumbra began, and remains, in a community center complex in the midst of the historically African American Rondo community in St. Paul. The theater was begun, partly, with federal dollars aimed at jobs and neighborhood development. Sarah Bellamy remembers, "Pillars of the black community were still living here and were involved in the community center with their children and grandchildren. They started coming to see the plays. We also had a lot of mixed families that were coming and a lot of white folks who were advocates for racial equity. I think this became a place where people could not only explore African American culture, but [also] maybe even imagine a more equitable future."

According to Lou Bellamy, "We produce, direct, choose, and present all of our work as though there were no one but African Americans in the audience. We know that isn't so. But it gives a certain kind of authenticity in the work. And it makes an audience that isn't in that culture sort of lean into the work, to do some work of their own, very much like we all have to do with Shakespeare. The audience extends their frame of reference by engaging with the art. When something has that authenticity and that ring of truth to it, it cuts across all cultures. That's what good art will always do."

The Twin Cities are home to other culturally specific and multicultural theaters as well. Teatro del Pueblo was founded in 1992 by Latino artists and community members on the West Side of St. Paul, in the heart of the city's Latino population. The theater serves primarily Latino work and artists, as well as both Latino and non-Latino patrons. It has staged more than fifty plays and toured to more than fifty schools throughout Minnesota. Artistic director Alberto Justiniano says his vision is for the theater "to become a portal into Latin America. I see Teatro and the arts as an opportunity for people to learn about other cultures, and as a tool for social change."

Pangea World Theater, under artistic director Dipankar Mukherjee, collaborates with international artists and companies to create plays and performances that speak across geography and culture. "Artists are seers of our communities," Mukherjee says, "giving voice to the world we envision." Pangea and Teatro del Pueblo have collaborated on Political Theatre Festival presentations and, beginning in 2014, the Latino Asian Fusion Series.

Director Lou Bellamy in rehearsal for *Big White Fog*, a co-presentation of Penumbra Theatre and the Guthrie Theater, with actor Abdul Salaam El-Razzac. (Photo courtesy of Penumbra Theatre)

Mukherjee says the theater's art form is influenced by both western and nonwestern vocabularies and styles in a complex way, describing Pangea's core artistic practices as inclusive since the theater's founding, "much before 'changing demographics' became a buzzword."

"Pangea," he goes on, "has worked to create and present stories from different communities for theater, changing our methods of auditioning in order to include artists from communities who are not trained in the traditional western methods of the audition process. Pangea uses diverse casts for all productions, and strives to bring a global and universally accessible literature to the theater. We are constantly striving to redefine and include aesthetic practices that emerge from the cultural aesthetics and styles of the artists that we collaborate with. From the very first encounter with artists, we realized that our own commitment to diversity demanded shifting our paradigms in order to create spaces in which different stories could be told and diverse voices could be heard."

For actor T. Mychael Rambo, places like Penumbra, Mu, and Teatro del Pueblo are reminders of how important it is to have audience members, benefactors, artists, and others "all wanting very much to hear and support the voices that are disenfranchised and marginalized. Minnesotans, at our core, live in that sort of identity. Each of those theaters play such truth and honesty and create such vivid, real, authentic portrayals of each of their specific cultural identities in ways that are not matched other places. That's beautiful to be able to have that. It happens because of audiences who want to see it and support it, and because they're able to harness the talent here that can provide those portrayals and those productions." When he arrived in Minnesota, Rambo says, "It was thrilling, it was enlivening to walk into a city and find a place where I saw myself in the room and on the stage."

The value in hearing the stories of the communities that live among us, stresses Randy Reyes, is that "society will be healthier. If you hear other people's stories, then you have compassion. If you have compassion, you'll be a better person. Fear goes away, and then you have an actual chance to live in harmony."

CHAPTER SEVEN

Process: Opening and Running

Preview performances and the workdays that accompany them can be among the longest days of theater work and the ones that require the most speed and agility. Rehearsals for *Chosen Play*, intense but still private, are over. When the stage manager announces that the house is open, everyone knows the public has arrived, and the weeks and months of work are about to be put to the test. From a backstage viewpoint, coming out of technical and dress rehearsals, all the complicated choreography and timing are still not fully routined for the crew. Will the mechanisms all work, the moving scenery, the costume quick changes, the prop handoffs, the special lighting effects, the rushing from place to place in the dark while the play moves inexorably forward? Don't miss that cue!

The same question, even more urgently, applies on stage: Will it *work*? Will the comic moments be funny, the dramatic moments have punch, the poignant moments be powerful? As the ears of the company are tuned to the reactions of the audience, the timing and rhythm of scenes and the story will flex. The first few moments, even the first few words, make it dazzlingly clear that the company is no longer alone in making the play. A moment that in rehearsal elicited cursory chuckles from the few people in the room might bring an explosion of laughter from the audience. The actor will need to let that laugh roll through the crowd before the scene can go on. The fight scene, so carefully choreographed, is making the audience gasp with tension and fear. Row upon row of seats are utterly still and silent for the monologue. Applause comes quickly, like a burst, at the end of the first act. How is it going? Is it working? How can we make it work *better*?

In the house, staff and creative teams can be glimpsed in the dark, yellow pads open for notes on what might and should be changed. After the show, out of costume, the company gathers in the seats to hear the news, both general and specific. They might be charged with excitement, or starting to sag with fatigue, or both—but the workday is not over. Each department has a chance to ask questions and make suggestions; decisions are made. It gets late. The designers and technicians make work lists and set start times for the following morning. The stage manager translates all the notes and information into a company work list and a call for the next afternoon's rehearsal. And then, the next day, it is done all over again.

"Preview week is a very intense period for us," says Children's Theatre Company's Peter Brosius. "We do three previews and open on a Friday, so

Sally Wingert and Tyler Michaels during a break from technical rehearsal for *Cabaret* with Theater Latté Da at the Pantages Theatre. Directed by Peter Rothstein, set design by Kate Sutton-Johnson, costume design by Rich Hamson, lighting design by Marcus Dilliard. (Photo by James Detmar)

we have Tuesday, Wednesday, Thursday, and Friday with four-hour days to work. We have reimagined entire shows, redesigned, restaged, we've re-choreographed numbers on Friday at 4:00 before a 7:00 opening. Because we know the hammer comes down, and if you haven't fixed it by opening night, if you haven't made those changes, it just rolls on."

No matter how much work and time and preparation you put into a production, nothing lives until it is presented to a live audience. "You can read the play, you can hear it read by actors, you can put it up on its feet in the rehearsal room," Brosius says, "but until it's in front of an audience, you don't really know what you have. It is the wildest and most alchemical art form. You get it in front of an audience and things that you thought were funny, touching, even brilliant in the rehearsal room reveal themselves to be something else sometimes. And then you've got to have the will and the team and the spirit to say, 'No, we're going to make massive and serious changes.' And it will be great and it will be fine and it will be better."

Boldness is required. Early in his tenure at the History Theatre in St. Paul, artistic director Ron Peluso remembers a new-work show by Syl Jones: *The Brotherhood.* With some trepidation, he attended the opening night dinner for donors without the playwright, who was at the theater rewriting the final scene. "I made my speech at the restaurant and left as soon as I could. When I got to the theater, I read the new scene, but it was too late. Up went the curtain, and that night, a brave cast delivered a new ending for the first time to an audience."

Eventually and inevitably, as Brosius says, the hammer comes down.

Opening Night: The Time Has Come

- ✓ *Writing the Play*
- ✓ *The Decision to Produce*
- ✓ *Assembling the Team*
- ✓ *Casting the Show*
- ✓ *Finding the Audience*
- ✓ *Rehearsing*
- ✓ *Technical and Dress Rehearsals*
- ✓ *Opening Night*

Opening nights in the theater are laden with tradition, symbolism, and weight that have been perpetuated over years. Flowers and gifts still pile up at the stage door. Family and friends arrive to honor the occasion. Board members and others dress up a notch, and so do solid citizens. Opening night parties are still held.

Some of the trappings of opening night, however, are now just a ghostly echo. These days critics do not all arrive on the same night, to be greeted in the lobby by publicity people, and then rush off to their city rooms to file their reviews in time for the next day's paper. Very few rotating searchlights reflect on the clouds above the Twin Cities.

From a backstage point of view, it might be argued that the more exciting moment is the first preview. "There's something thrilling about that first night," says actor T. Mychael Rambo about the moment when the first audience files in and takes their seats. "It's the first time you really meet the rest of the ensemble. It's like your guest star has just arrived."

The interplay between the ensemble and the audience is the very stuff of the theater. This energy, live energy, is in a constant state of flux, and no matter how long you have rehearsed, the presence of the audience makes it all different.

"I was taught you have to be connected to the audience's rhythms," says actor Bradley Greenwald. "You are in a state of communication with them. If you're doing a comedy, for example, you can't be doing the next punch line over people's laughter. That's cheating the material, and yourself, and cheating the audience of another moment of enjoyment."

Greenwald continues, "If you're doing something where suddenly the audience gets very still because they're listening so hard, you don't want to destroy that sense of connection. When you get the sudden sensation that they are hanging on every word, that can change the rhythm of how you're going to lead them to the next part. You don't want to leave them behind."

Previews lead to openings, and opening nights are a marker in the fluid cycle of theater making, and a fine excuse to celebrate. This may be the first time that the designers have a chance to relax enough to see the whole project together, without the daily pressure of improving it. Costume designer Rich Hamson says, "There's nothing better than seeing an opening night where everything comes together, when you finally see all the pictures in your head. And when all the elements work, it's like going to church when I was a kid, that strange kind of spirituality thing. It's like doing a painting and then looking at that canvas. For costumes, it never finishes until the audience."

Artistic director Randy Reyes also believes in the magnitude of opening nights: "I think openings are what it's all about," he says. "It's a birth of something, another step, another milestone. It's for the whole community to celebrate a beginning, in a series of beginnings."

For some directors and designers, opening night is the last day of work. "What happens to me when the audience arrives," says Jungle Theater's Bain Boehlke, "is the most profound sense of cosmic blues, of no longer being necessary. If the director has been doing his or her job, he's been the audience, creating the play the audience will be able to ride in. When they come, you, who are the most knowledgeable lover of the work, are now supplanted."

Openings can provide a jolt of energy as friends, colleagues, and family arrive for the big night. Sometimes special guests bring special atmosphere with them. Ron Peluso remembers a show he commissioned at the History Theatre about the orphan trains, which operated between 1858 and 1928 to transport hundreds of thousands of homeless immigrant children from the East to Midwest farm families. "On opening night, we had eight men and women, orphan riders now in their eighties and nineties, sitting in the front row, and before the curtain went up, I interviewed them on stage. One gentleman had been separated from his sister when the trains stopped in Albert Lea, Minnesota. She was taken by her new family to Iowa; they found each other in a joyful reunion forty years later."

"In our play," Peluso remembers, "there was a similar scenario, a brother and sister separated and then reunited. At the curtain call, the gentleman from Albert Lea walked up to the stage and hugged the two young actors who'd played the brother and sister; the crowd rose up and cheered— cheers and tears both." Openings at the History Theatre, says Peluso, often have either the real people or their relatives sitting in the house. He often watches the audience more than the play on openings.

Playing conditions vary, particularly early in the run. Previews are perilous and can be full of change, and sometimes attract only small houses, which can be deceptive in terms of audience reaction. Openings are often filled

History Theatre artistic director Ron Peluso *(right)* on stage with former vice president Walter Mondale in a post-show discussion of *1968: The Year That Rocked the World.* (Photo by Karen Mueller)

with friends and supporters—a suddenly much bigger house—and the atmosphere can be decidedly friendly. Stage manager Chris Code calls opening night audiences "completely outside the norm. Their reactions are much quicker and larger than the average group of patrons." Sometimes a show does not settle down until a few performances into the run, when the playing conditions become more predictable.

From a backstage viewpoint, openings can be quite the opposite of a special night. Code says, "By the time we get there at the Guthrie, we've had five previews along with five days of rehearsal to make all the tweaks and fixes, so we know the show very, very well. Opening night is rather anticlimactic backstage, with a sense of relief that we have moved on from the rehearsal phase and into the known world of performances."

After the show, lobbies and rehearsal rooms are filled with tables of appetizers and temporary cocktail bars, both humble and posh. Actors in their dressing rooms do their own quick change, out of costume and into party clothes. Gifts are exchanged, cards are written. Some of the gifts are saved as memorabilia. Some of the cards are sincere and full of goodwill and friendship.

And some are not. There's a tale of a long-past theater conflict that came to a lawsuit. A witness was presented with the opening night card he'd sent the plaintiff, a note of congratulations and admiration. "Right here," says the lawyer, reading, "you tell him he was great and you appreciated his work. Now you say he did a terrible job; how can that be?" The witness, with a strongly dismissive gesture, says, "It's an opening night card—everybody just lies!"

For those going on with the run, playing a show presents a different set of challenges from rehearsing and opening, an entirely different rhythm and pace. Beyond the occasional understudy or brush-up work, there are no rehearsals. The stage manager takes on maintenance of the show, most importantly as a steady, ongoing set of eyes, closely watching the workings of the complicated mechanism and giving feedback. *Chosen Play* is in the hands of the actors and the audience—and the audience changes every night.

Anyone who has ever participated in a run of shows longer than four or five performances knows that each one, while the same, is in some sense utterly different. It has to be. Even once a show has settled into a routine, it still has many moving parts, both mechanical and human. The addition of the audience brings a wild card of energy every time, and professional standards demand that the performance be kept fresh for every audience. Each performance is, after all, brand new to every audience.

Boehlke reflects on the role of the audience: "I think the audience plays the most significant role in keeping a play fresh. The audience doesn't come to watch a play, it comes to participate, and it is the other half of a production. Theater is player and audience. It does not exist in the rehearsal space. Since the audience is what makes theater, then the play is always fresh because the players are always listening to the audience."

Actor Bradley Greenwald observes that each audience has its own chemistry and its own psychology: "You don't know until you're in front of that audience what their chemistry is. Do they tend to be a really quiet audience; do you have to scale back the shouting? . . . If they're listening really hard, you don't need to be as big because you know you've got their attention. You're going out on a date with the audience each time, and you don't know their chemistry until you start the date."

"The audience has a lot of control," says actor H. Adam Harris. "If only we could teach a class about how much control you really exert as an audience member. We love those audible intakes and those breaths. I think the theater is always about the audience. People sometimes say you can do theater anywhere. Yes, but a person has to be there to witness it!"

"We are aware of [audience members]," says Greenwald. "And we need them. We all need to be in the same room. They're not watching a movie, and we're not in a rehearsal room; we're all there together, which is the beauty of communally shared performing arts."

A query often heard around curtain time in any theater is, "How's the house?" Apparent meanings can vary: How big is the audience? Is there a lot of gray hair, or is it skewing younger? If the performance is a student show, are they attentive or likely to be noisy? In the language of the theater, "how's the house" can also address more elemental concerns: Are audience members listening? Are they going to commune with us? What do they *feel* like?

[The Guthrie's thrust stage is] the most exciting theater space I have ever been in, in my life. You walk out; it's relatively small, but you are the focal point of this surround-sound of humanity. The way that space feels when all those people are there doing an energy exchange with you—that's the true high of it. The audience is another character that you're communicating with. So you get revved. You get charged. If the audience is willing to come in with sort of an open heart, it's just juicy! You just thrum!

—ACTOR SALLY WINGERT

Sometimes you don't know until the curtain goes down, notes H. Adam Harris. "At the end of the play they tell you with their applause. They tell you whether they enjoyed it, or what it meant. They tell you what they felt. And they tell you sometimes about how they're going to exit and what they're going to do with the experience."

Harris likes to walk out through the lobby after performances, especially at the Children's Theatre Company, where, in 2014, he played eighty-four performances as Max the dog in *How the Grinch Stole Christmas.* "Those kids are like no other audiences. I go down on one knee and talk to them on their level. 'Did you have a good time? Did you enjoy the show? Oh my goodness, it's your first play? Well, here I am, I'm an actor. It's not a movie; I'm here, I'm real.'"

At Penumbra, co–artistic director Sarah Bellamy enjoys standing in the house during performances. "I love to watch the audience watch the play. I love seeing them lean forward, I love seeing their brows furrow. I love it when they erupt in laughter. I love it when I see someone pull a Kleenex from their purse. And I love watching them leave the theater, when I can see how they've reacted. They're usually very talkative, or they're really silent because they are emotionally processing."

"A theater production is only half-evolved without the audience," Bellamy continues. "Every night it's a new and different play because the people in the space change it. You need everybody there, and it really feels like a communal experience."

Costume designer Sonya Berlovitz loves opening nights, but she also always goes back to see her shows during the run: "I like to see how the show has grown. I like the chance to just relax and look at it as an audience member. I also think it's helpful to me as a designer; it's a chance for self-reflection about what I've done to it."

Actor Anna Sundberg tells people to come see a show during its closing week: "I feel like I grow so much and keep discovering throughout the course of a run. When you think about it, a three- or four-week run is not a very long time to get to know the person you're playing. Sometimes rehearsal is a little bit more of a skeleton, and then in performance all the muscle and sinews and ligaments come in. I always think a show's better on the closing than it is at the opening."

Sundberg played 101 performances as Maid Marian in the Children's Theatre Company's *Robin Hood* in 2014. She says, "It's a testament to the complexity of the show when, at 101 performances, you're still discovering things. I loved that show, and I felt I was completely present for every one."

How can she repeat a performance night after night throughout a run? "Because that's the job," she says with a smile.

Anna Sundberg as Maid Marian, with Dean Holt and company, in *Robin Hood* at Children's Theatre Company. (Photo by Dan Norman)

CHAPTER EIGHT

The Twin Cities: Why Theater People Come and Stay

> *A marvelous convenient place for our rehearsal. This green*
> *plot shall be our stage,*
> *this hawthorn-brake our tiring house.*
>> —William Shakespeare, *A Midsummer Night's Dream*

Sometimes a long lens is necessary to see the difference between individual decisions and larger movement. Hard work that engages the mind and spirit, and has unbreakable deadlines, is absorbing; it does not always allow space for perspective. Each person who makes up part of the Twin Cities theater community arrived somehow, found their work somehow, somehow continues their part of the work, and such decisions, though formative, can seem quite small. On reflection, these individual moments, in aggregate, result in movement toward a community large and vital enough to support theater artists, and also to attract more. Momentum is involved, and critical mass, and tipping points. Serendipity and intention. Ripples that start in one place and travel to the edge of a pond. A creative rising tide that, somehow, lifts a wide variety of boats.

In an onstage conversation at the Guthrie Theater, moderated by Jeremy Cohen, freelance director Joel Sass talked about his own decision: "When I graduated from college in the late eighties, there was an expectation that in order to find legitimacy and validation, to get your toe-picks into the glacier of a career, you really need to move to one of the coasts. I'm really grateful that I resisted that."

Sass owes that decision to one conversation: "Someone said to me, 'Really? Have you bought that story? Why do you think that you need to be a theater artist based in New York or Los Angeles or Chicago?' No, I thought. This country is large enough. Don't we need good artists elsewhere? Aren't there smart audiences everywhere? And actors here and there and everywhere? Do you think you're doing it for prestige, or a perception of a certain degree of exposure? Or are you doing it so you can be embedded in a community of artists and an audience who will share those stories?"

Sass found that community in the Twin Cities and started his own venture, Mary Worth Theatre Company, in 1994. He reflects, "I stayed here because the ecology of the Twin Cities was such that a young person coming out of college and choosing not to go into debt for graduate school could take those resources and plow them into self-production. You could find a like-minded series of colleagues and create a company. It was possible to put together some resources, get some small grants, and live a fairly decent life, and learn how to design or build or compose, or paint or sculpt or write. And we could do it in a place where an audience would gather around it—and critics would come to review it."

Sass kept his Mary Worth Theatre Company going for nine years before moving on to other work. Looking back on the experience, he says, "It gave me eight or nine years when I didn't have to ingratiate myself and absorb the aesthetic of other people who could give me a job. It forced me to

To young directors: You need to be making work. Find a play that really speaks to you. Find a number of people it really speaks to, too, and get yourself into a damned basement, garage, bar, or back alley. Put on that damned show.

—DIRECTOR AND DESIGNER JOEL SASS

encounter my own aesthetic, to find my own voice. It taught me to work with artists who had all come from different disciplines, who came with different training vocabularies. And we were able to do it all ourselves."

His assessment: "For someone who is wondering how to get to San Francisco or New York or LA, you realize that if you're really serious about doing theater, it's not about where you go. It's about the caliber of your collaboration and how effectively you can engage with the audience."

This bracing observation runs counter to a powerful mythos about the U.S. coasts, particularly the East Coast, that is not confined to the world of the theater. Like most stereotypes, it is built around a grain of truth. The high paychecks, the great glitz, and the pace of New York—and one's ability to survive there—can provide a kind of lifelong cachet. Being known as a "New York actor" can persist long after that actor's departure from New York City. Another phrase is "New York–based," which can mean that you ostensibly live in the city, where so many theaters go to hold their auditions, but most or all of your work is elsewhere.

New York is thrilling, no question, but what does that mean about having a career, or a life?

"Some people move to the Twin Cities because it is way more livable than New York," says director Rick Shiomi. "You're constantly under pressure to succeed there. Everybody's hustling something. Now there are good things to that, but there are bad things, too, in terms of one's personal life, and lifestyle and livability quotient. If you're in New York, it's so competitive. There are like a hundred people there for every person in theater here. And with a hundred people trying to get the same job, rather than five people, it's so competitive. It's the same in LA. Everybody is so intent on their own individual career. Forget about companies, because in LA theater companies are serving the purpose of showcasing actors so they can get into TV and films."

Actor Ricardo Vazquez's family lives in Minneapolis, but he applied a practical filter to his decision to stay in the Twin Cities after working on the East Coast. "What made the Twin Cities the location and the place for me," he says, "was the amount of opportunities that are available. I had to think of my own self as a small little entity running a business. I had to make business decisions based off what business was available and what business wasn't."

Vazquez found work in Minneapolis and was introduced to artistic directors from Pangea World Theater and Teatro del Pueblo, who were collaborating on *Oedipus El Rey*. Of the title character in that play, Vazquez notes, "It was an amazing role for a young Latino actor." He recalls that a friend told him, "You know, you could stay here and you would be one of the Latino actors in this city and you can do this role. Or you can go to New York and you would be in the pool again of thousands of Latino actors and there's still only that one role. What do you want to do? Do you want to play the role or do you want to wait in line?"

"At that point, it all sunk in," says Vazquez. "My work can be just as successful to me in this city as it can be anywhere. At the end of the day, my work and what I put into it has to be owned by me." He recognized that he needed to be in charge of his own opportunities and challenges.

Designer Kate Sutton-Johnson was hired by the Guthrie to work in their prop department before she graduated from college, where most of her classmates were "really hot to go to New York. But I just had this intuition that it was not the right fit for me. I felt that I might thrive more somewhere else. And I didn't want to be an assistant for years and years. In my mind, that was the life of becoming a designer in New York, to really pay your dues for a decade or more before you could really do your own work. Now, assisting people is very valuable, but I really wanted to start designing my own stuff as soon as possible."

She had first gone to Chicago to meet with key people in the community there and get some advice, but she walked away from those appointments feeling discouraged. "My overall impression was that they were sort of saying, 'Well yeah, you can move here if you want. But I don't have any job opportunities for you and you can't really expect much to happen when you're just out of school. So you can move here, but you're just going to have to find your way. Good luck.' There was no tangible way in. There wasn't the sort of generous spirit that I found here."

The "generous spirit" theme permeates the tales of many theater people based in the Twin Cities. Sutton-Johnson met many people in the theater community through her position renting Guthrie props to other theaters, but she left the Guthrie after two seasons because she was anxious to start designing sets and "didn't want to get labeled as the prop girl; if people get to know you in one way, it can be hard to escape that when you want someone to recognize you as a designer."

Sutton-Johnson went to interview with Jack Reuler at Mixed Blood Theatre, and "he handed me every script that he was doing that season and said, 'Do as many as you want.' That happened to me everywhere. I was a young designer and I hadn't had a lot of work produced. I was just amazed that I was given so many opportunities."

For anyone who works in the theater, artistic director Peter Rothstein says there is always a magnet to New York: "You feel that pull; listen to that. But also evaluate the notion of *being* in New York versus *working* in New York. If you have work where you are that is fueling your soul, that is building your résumé, you should seriously evaluate whether you want to walk away from that work, in hopes of work in New York. Right out of grad school, half my colleagues moved to New York City, and a year later, one of them was excited because he'd finally landed one commercial. I had done four productions. That was very affirming for the choice that I made."

Artistic director Michelle Hensley founded her theater, Ten Thousand Things, in Los Angeles in 1991 and ran it there for several years. "But then I had a child," she says. "Los Angeles is not a place to raise a child; at least it seemed to me to be very, very hard. So my husband at the time and I were looking for a place where we could afford to buy a house as two freelancers, we could use the public schools, and there was a vibrant theater community. And that narrowed it down to the Twin Cities."

Costume designer Rich Hamson speaks frankly about why he settled in the Twin Cities: "I spent about six months in New York, and what I discovered is it's much easier to be poor in [Minneapolis], and you can live a good life. I don't mean dirt poor, but you can live on so much less and have a better quality of life here. You really can learn to live inexpensively and have a home here. And there's so much stuff going on."

Jesse Cogswell, a lighting designer who graduated in 2013, notes another difference between New York and the Twin Cities: "When I went to visit

Lighting designer Jesse Cogswell working as master electrician at the Great River Shakespeare Festival in Winona, Minnesota. (Photo by Stacy McKenney)

New York for the Design East showcase," he recalls, "I showed my business card, which has all four things listed—programming, drafting, electrician work, and design. And they said, 'No. You don't want to do that. You want a different business card for each one because if you give that to a producer, the producer is going to think you're not really any of them, you're just a generalist. You're not serious enough to hire as a designer.'"

"I understand the point," Cogswell says. "But I do all four fairly well. I love doing all of it, the electrician work, drafting, programming, all of it feeds different needs. And this town has big opportunities to do all of that. The variety is really incredible, so that in the course of a day, I can draft a light plot, hang somebody else's light plot, and then design on my own. I don't feel like I need to be pigeonholed into one slot, and it seems like that's kind of rare."

Being pigeonholed is related to being typecast, something actor Anna Sundberg feels strongly about. She says, "That's one incredibly wonderful thing about working here: I don't get typecast here. I pride myself on being versatile and I like to play all kinds of different characters, and I feel like I have that ability. If I moved to Hollywood tomorrow, they would be like, 'Well, who is she? She's not pretty enough to be the pretty girl and not ugly enough to be the ugly girl. She's sort of funny, but also kind of serious. We don't know where to put her.'"

Peter Rothstein adds a directorial viewpoint: "One thing I hear a lot from colleagues in New York—actors, designers—is that they tend to get pigeonholed. They can only do musical theater, they can only do realism, they can only do the African American stories. I think this community thrives on people who can cross over, who are multidisciplinary.... You can see actor Greta Oglesby in August Wilson and then see her in *Caroline, or Change*. Then go to a cabaret where she's performing, and then read her book. The audience here aligns themselves with artists who do that cross-over work, and I think that's quite extraordinary."

Sometimes such versatility and range of talent is on view within a single show. As Bradley Greenwald says, "It's very hard now to go to a show here where you don't have actors, professionally trained singers, dancers, and instrumentalists all on stage. It's not actors on the stage, instrumentalists in the pit, and dancers coming out for intermezzi between scenes. They're all on stage together and what they're making is what those talents and imaginations can do in that moment, with crossover disciplines."

Rothstein believes that the Minnesota Fringe Festival, by providing a venue for actors to put on works as a writer or producer, has had a tremendous impact on actors feeling they can have a voice. "Not only are they not pigeonholed, but [also] people are celebrated for the ability to cross over. Being a writer or designer *and* a storyteller *and* an actor *and* a dancer; I think that makes actors who are more well-rounded. It makes actors have a voice, because they've been called upon to have a point of view beyond the rehearsal room. Of course you have a point of view as an actor, but sometimes you can think more holistically about the work, when you've had the opportunity to be in the driver's seat in various capacities. I do think that is unique to this city."

Another point that makes the Twin Cities community notable, Rothstein continues, "is that we are artists and citizens here. So many cities in this country do all their casting out of New York City. That's the notion of a group of total strangers arriving and they live in a generic corporate apartment. They work in a rehearsal room that has no vestige of the history that came before. They spend two months and then they get back on the plane and the cleaners come through and another group arrives. They aren't part of our churches, their children aren't in our schools, they're not part of the political movements locally. I do think that has a tremendous impact both on leading a life that is full and complete, and on the work itself. . . . I don't think there are many cities in this country that have this size theater community where they live, work, and engage in the social fabric of the place."

The Twin Cities seem peculiarly hospitable to the rare notion that you can have a career in the theater and also have a life. "I had to decide I wanted a life," says playwright Kira Obolensky, "and I had to make a really conscious decision to do that. So if you define 'life' as having a home, having a garden, developing interests outside your career, I do. I think if I lived in New York or in Los Angeles and were on that kind of path, I don't think I would be able to do all the cool things I do. It's time and money, time and money. I don't need that much money to live, you know? I look at various friends who live in other places in the country and this is just the darn truth of it. They have to make twice as much money as I do to have the same standard of living."

Obolensky also cherishes the creative time and space that is available in the Twin Cities. She reflects, "There is the opportunity here to actually say, 'Okay, well, there isn't anything here so let's just do it.' I think it has to do with pace of life. It doesn't take you forty-five minutes to mail a letter. You don't have to commute forever on a subway into a job. We have lives that are somewhat in place, so we have time. I don't think there's room in New York for a lot of new ventures; that's because the stakes are so high and the cost of living is so high. You can invent and reinvent [in Minnesota]. There's a convergence of a sense of possibility and a sense of tradition."

Some people like to work all the time, and some people have no life outside of their work; this is hardly unique to the creative life. But artists nearly always want to make something better, and most arts projects can always be made better, or at least closer to the originator's vision. This leaves the door open to working all the time. The demands of the theater require an intentional choice to step away if one is going to claim a life outside of work.

Balance can be a goal. As actor Tyler Michaels asserts, "To be able to maintain a personal life is important. I think that makes us better artists in some way. You have to experience your own personal life to bring something to the table theatrically. Of course, you can just be without those experiences and just do theater, theater, theater, and perhaps be a genius. Or perhaps be crazy. Maybe those are one and the same. But I would like to be one of those geniuses who's not crazy, who has a life and is an innovator of theater, too. Something that allows new people who come to the community to say what can I do? Sort of open doors for other people."

Lighting designer Marcus Dilliard, who moved to the Twin Cities from Boston for a job at the Guthrie in the 1980s, knew early on that balance was a goal: "As much as I love this, I need to get away from it on a very practical level in order for it not to become tedious or all-consuming."

"When we were here for a year," Dilliard remembers, "we started looking around and saying 'wow.' Maybe we should just buy a house. We can always sell it in a year or two if we decide to leave, because it was really easy to buy a house. The one we got needed a fair amount of work, and that was an outlet, just a way to sort of disengage the brain and do something manual. There were houses that were affordable for young couples, and it was pretty clear early on that, unlike Boston or New York, this was a city where it was possible, easy, to have children and not have to live an hour outside of town. There were neighborhoods and we were five minutes away from the Guthrie. I could run to work if I had to. It was a community where people had a lot of respect for your life outside your career. I'm talking about people in the business, and outside the business, too. . . . The overall outlook on life that you find here is that your career is your career, and it's important, but it really shouldn't be everything that you do."

"And there is longevity and stability here, too," Dilliard adds. "I have thirty years of work history with colleagues in this community. How many other places could that happen?"

Does he ever regret his choice to settle here?

"No. No—only when it's really, really cold."

Winter is a dominant theme in the Upper Midwest, both positive and negative. Penumbra Theatre's Sarah Bellamy travels all over the country and speaks with people in other communities. "When I say I'm from the Twin Cities, if they understand the theater, they all want to get here! Or they've come here and had a great experience in the theater."

Then she adds, smiling, "They just can't come in February. Then they won't stay."

Joel Sass credits the landscape and climate of Minnesota for doing much to feed the artistic soul: "It's the cycle of the seasons, which are so undeniable. Almost in a Nordic sense, there's the dark winter, which forces a degree of artistic theological introspection, which I'm not inclined to in sunnier locales.... The fact that we can be in the middle of the city and twenty minutes later be out on a lake feels very Arcadian and Chekovian to me."

The cultural and social environment is just as important as the natural and geographic, Sass adds. "Having watched its progression for the twenty years I've been here, the city has a museum and café and music and restaurant and cultural scene which is extraordinary. It's becoming more diverse than one would imagine a midwestern community could be; there's so much work ahead in terms of meeting the responsibility of that and the opportunity of that. Being part of that excites me."

Even though the theater is "a constant struggle," Sass says, "and we always feel somewhat at risk, most of us have had for twenty years the ability to have a creative life, to be married or partnered, in some cases to have children, and both be working in a creative field. And have, if we choose, a home and a mortgage in a city that affords a nice quality of life. The amenities of being in an urban forest in one of the greatest green-space-ratioed cities in America, with access to not only the arts institutions that house the work we do but [also] all the sister and brother organizations of dance and music and world-class museums. It's been really great to see."

A life in the theater, frequently precarious in income and stability, can make the decision to have a child a tough one, even in a theater-hospitable town like the Twin Cities. The hours are long and out of sync with most of the work world; the level of childcare coverage needed will be high. Actor Sally Wingert raised two children and never stopped working. "There were things that were helpful," she says. "First, I had peers that were having children. My friend Barbara Kingsley had her first child while we were company members at Actors Theatre of St. Paul. I saw that she continued to work and all of it. We had a joke as young mothers, and I know young actresses say it now: 'I'm pregnant; I'll never work again.' It's such a lie. It doesn't work like that. . . . You don't stop being a good actor because you're a mom. I say au contraire. I became a much better actor. You can choose not to work anymore, but if you were working before you got pregnant, you will be working after you have a child."

People were not always aware of the effort required and the exhaustion that she lived with in the dual role of being a young mother while acting at the Guthrie, but, she acknowledges, "I was paid well. I bought a house. I drove a car. I was living a very middle-class life. Of course, my children were well cared for because I had a husband who was absolutely an equal partner in parenting. My parents lived here and that helped. It's the same with any person, I think, going into a career in the face of parenthood; certainly any woman has to cope with this."

What I say to young actors when they talk about marriage and kids: You just have to leap into the void. The moment will never be exactly right.

—ACTOR SALLY WINGERT

Wingert continues, "I think a hallmark of my work is an emotional intelligence, and I feel that comes from a full life. My husband and children have aided me; they fill up the well. They've given me trials and tribulations and joy and just all kinds of things that I'm then able to tap and know, in a kind of emotional wisdom as an actor."

Michelle Hensley notes that, in her generation, there were very few women directors who had children, and it remains a challenge for women today. When she settled her company in the Twin Cities, the supportive creative atmosphere became even more important to the development of both her professional and her personal life. She chose a very specific path, and, she says, "I still get young woman directors coming to me, saying,

'How do you do it?' I can only tell them, 'Start your own company.' When you start your own company, you set the parameters. If you want a life and do theater, you should find a way to start your own company, even if you're not a director. Or find a group of like-minded people to join with, because as a freelancer, you are at the whim of institutions that do not yet accommodate family life."

Think hard and deep about why you want to [be in theater], and how you want to do it. Think about what you don't like about the theater right now and how it operates, and what you can do to change it. Make it up for yourself; the theater needs enormous reinventing in our country.

—ARTISTIC DIRECTOR MICHELLE HENSLEY

Another sign of the health and vitality of the theater scene in the Twin Cities is that theatrical activity is a recognized part of the community—touted, appreciated, and part of the public conversation. It appears in our media, is regularly featured in newspapers, radio, and television in more than just a review format. Work in the arts is lifted up publicly as being important to the quality of life in our state and region. Artists' work lives are recognized work lives. The mayors of both Twin Cities use words like *amazing*, *vibrant*, and *tremendous* when describing the theatrical community.

Playwright Kira Obolensky believes that the respect afforded to artists and theater people in the Twin Cities is not necessarily found in other communities. "There are certain places in the country where I just say I'm a writer," she explains, "because if you define yourself as a playwright, you might just as well have announced that you make your own shoes. But here in the Cities, I can say I'm a playwright. I think that's because there's such a good theater community and such good people. People even know there's such a thing as a Playwrights' Center."

Locating a home, especially an artistic home, can be an accidental process or a deliberate one. Playwright Carlyle Brown was searching for an artistic home and found one, to his surprise, in the Twin Cities. He says, "I've been fortunate. I've had work. I lived a playwright's life on a national scene, and spent a lot of years doing my work. But always in airplanes, hotel rooms. They're all alike. Going to rehearsals, starting off in a room full of strangers and doing the show for an audience that you'll never see again. There was something about it that lacked continuity in terms of developing

Playwright and actor Carlyle Brown at work in his writing studio. (Photo by Barbara Rose-Brown)

as an artist. People talked about community, but I wasn't really quite sure what that was. My community was spread out to all the four winds."

Brown gradually began to realize that he was in search of an artistic home, and the existence of creative allies made all the difference. "To my surprise, when I looked around, I realized the home I was looking for wasn't a theater, but a place, like the Twin Cities," he says. "And when you're working with old friends, everything about it is efficient, artistically. We get in a room, we sit at a table, we know each other. We can just get to work. It's a process like collaborative procreation."

"The generosity of the community of artists here," Brown continues, "is just astounding. That's what makes things happen. Your lighting designer being able to borrow lights or some kind of gizmo from another theater. A prop designer splitting stuff they use on gigs. Advice and encouragement. Using the same designers. We get each other and we like each other and we hang out together. I guess it's not really strange; before the emergence of the director that's how it worked for Shakespeare and Molière. After a while we know what each other is talking about. They know what we want, we know what we're getting at. We know what we can do to make it alive."

Mixed Blood artistic director Jack Reuler describes the theater community in the Twin Cities as being almost like a mythical creature: "Everybody else has heard about it and they've been told how amazing it is. But they've never really witnessed it. But in reality, we are a unicorn."

Reuler, echoing Brown's assessment of the generosity and collegiality in the Twin Cities theater community, says that the people really get along with one another: "They really look out for each other's well-being. There isn't backstabbing. There's no stratification or hierarchy. The Guthrie and Walking Shadow and Mixed Blood and Penumbra and Yellow Tree are all lateral partners, doing what they do at different scales. They're working together so what we have to offer is a broad spectrum of aesthetics, of missions, and of what theater can do."

"I think the biggest part of the unicorn," Reuler continues, "is just the congenial and collegial nature of the various organizations. There are dynamic struggles within them, but there is actually a spirit of generosity that overrides it. That spirit manifests itself in people helping people find opportunities for employment, for artistic expression, and for venues and also in the sharing of props and costumes and scenery and sound equipment and media equipment. There's no sense of 'I have something you don't, and therefore you should want what I have.' It's, 'If I have it, you should use it.'"

Theater is, however, hardly a perfect world. Making a life and making a living in the theater is a challenge anywhere, and that includes the Twin Cities, however deeply embedded the community is in civic life, however many theaters professional and amateur, however many good education programs and training opportunities.

Some limitations are endemic to the Twin Cities and even more are a general condition of the profession. The rich theatrical field, however touted and true, can present more opportunities for audiences than practitioners. Like other places, the Twin Cities still has many more people who want to perform than there are performance opportunities, especially ones that come with a paycheck. The business of film production and radio and television work in the Twin Cities, especially voice-overs, has fallen off in recent years; that work used to be another possible income stream for actors. The national recession that began in 2008 hit many theaters, and many theater artists, hard. Workweeks are not abundant, and well-paid workweeks are even rarer. Staff and associate jobs exist in our institutional structures, but staff jobs can severely limit the artistic freedoms of the freelance life. Day jobs are a necessity for many theater people. Artists who are recognized members of this community may find it easier to find work than those just arriving.

Theater has never been easy, even if one disregards the often insoluble problem of making a good show, as opposed to just getting one up at all. Jack Reuler, whose family has been in the Twin Cities for five generations and who has worked in theater since 1976, observes, "For all the people that come and make a living here, there are people that come and stop making a living at it. The people who've really been able to make a life and make a living in the Twin Cities are the tip of the iceberg. There are a huge number of people who've made an avocational life in the theater, or an academic life in the theater, or who have left the theater. That number is much larger."

Very true. People teach theater, and make it, in our extended system of colleges and universities and high schools, both private and public. People work and volunteer in our large and longstanding network of community theaters, creating as wide a range of work as in the professional realm and often pouring in just as much heart and effort. Theater advocates serve on boards of directors, lobby for public support, write donor checks to their favorite institutions, and stand public witness to the central and natural place of the arts in their lives.

And, perhaps most importantly, they attend the theater as patrons. Any typical audience, of whatever size, in any Twin Cities theater contains a constellation of enthusiasts, each having arrived in that particular seat on that particular night for their own reason. When the lights go down and the stage comes up, the presence of those receptive ears and eyes completes the circuit, and the show can go on.

Tyler Michaels had a star turn as the Emcee in Theater Latté Da's production of *Cabaret* in 2014, and at that year's Ivey Awards, he opened the show with the "Willkommen" number, sung as he was lowered on a trapeze over the stage of the State Theatre packed with two thousand theater folk and fans, dressed to the nines and wildly enthusiastic. I asked him what he saw when he looked out over the house.

"The feeling, the energy of it, was (pardon my language), 'fuck, yeah!' This is us. We are we. This is our community and we are making it strong and we are making it stronger by doing this. Celebratory, congratulatory, fuck yeah kind of energy. You could feel the creative energy bubbling underneath. It is at moments like the Iveys where you think, 'There is so much happening and I want to make it even better. I want to be part of the next thing that makes the Twin Cities the place to be.' It felt like a call to arms, like, 'Let's keep going, let's go even further. We ain't stopping now.' I want to be part of that, and to be a part of that in this community."

Tyler Michaels as the Emcee during tech rehearsal for Theater Latté Da's *Cabaret*, directed by Peter Rothstein. Set design by Kate Sutton-Johnson, costume design by Rich Hamson, lighting design by Marcus Dilliard. (Photo by James Detmar)

CHAPTER NINE

Process: Taking Your Seat

The journey of *Chosen Play* from writing to production to running is a long arc of effort from theater workers who bring their individual skills and passions and opinions to the many different facets of creating the work. Eventually all decisions are made; the show is settled. The audience arrives to complete the circle.

And what about the audience's journey to the curtain? Each individual who takes his or her seat before the lights go down has made a choice to see a particular show; the Twin Cities offers a rich buffet of possibilities. The show is being presented for you; your presence is requested and required. The theater professionals are presenting their chosen play. How do you choose?

Let us, for the moment, disregard the wealth of other ways Twin Citians can spend their time and money. Disregard the museums and galleries; the film houses and movies; the pleasures of the outdoors; the dance world; the poetry, both slam and traditional; the very rich and complex music scene; the clubs. Put aside, for the moment, the author readings and lectures and the wealth of presentations associated with our colleges and universities. Put out of your mind the sports scene—professional, amateur, collegiate, baseball, football, basketball, soccer, and everything else. Don't think about the citywide festivals and neighborhood celebrations, or the lure of lakes and zoos and parks and band shells.

No. You're going to the theater.

Let us also stipulate that few among the audience are so fortunate as to have unlimited entertainment dollars to spend. All or nearly all of us want to choose wisely, to avoid wasting the night out or the money, both of which can be scarce and precious. You've decided you have the time and you're ready to buy the ticket. But what do you want to see? On any given night, you might have several dozen options, and every one of those presenters very much wants your presence in their audience.

They're trying to reach you, and perhaps some of that has gotten through. There are print ads in newspapers and magazines. There are online ads. There are radio ads and mentions. There are mailings. There are banners and signage on the venues themselves. There are ads in the skyways, and on buses and trains, and ad partnerships with restaurants and workplaces. All or most of the presenters have websites and Facebook pages, where they have posted promos and short videos; social media use is effective, direct, and cheap. You might have read some feature articles. Most buy advertising in each other's printed programs, when they can afford the space or can trade. Nothing about this is accidental. Smart professionals are working hard to appeal to you through all these available conduits; one or more of them might have succeeded in catching your eye.

Many factors go into your decision—some conscious, some unconscious, all viable and worthy. You might know the title. Some theaters put celebrities on stage; you might recognize the name of the star of the show. You might have heard about the show around the water cooler, or you may be taking the tried and true route of relying on a friend to decide. You might have been lured by a discount offer.

The fact remains that the theater in the Twin Cities is a complex and buzzing community, and there's more to see than can be seen. How do you sort out the options? How do you make your sampling intentional as opposed to accidental? How do you deepen your experience, have the most fun, not miss something wonderful? Here are a few suggestions for navigating the scene and getting the most out of the Twin Cities' rich and diverse theatrical offerings.

- First and best, find someone to follow. The Twin Cities are well populated with freelance artists who move all the time from job to job; you have encountered many of them in this book. An actor's work year might include a lead role at the Jungle, a supporting part at the Guthrie, a new script at Illusion, an appearance at Park Square, and more. Follow the actor, and you'll be astonished by the transformations he or she makes. Many performers have webpages which announce their upcoming schedule.

- Or, find another kind of artist to follow. Choose a design area of interest to you and follow a particular designer. How can such a wide variety of costume styles, or scenery, or lights spring from one person's brain? Try following a director's work shaping entire worlds on the stage; his or her aesthetic is on display in a different setting each time.

- Follow a playwright, choosing several of his or her plays to see and think about. With new work, hear a script read in development and then hear it again in a full production. Read it; then read it aloud. What do you think the playwright is saying through the play? What do you think they think?

- Find a theater company to follow. Many filters are available. You can choose one that's close to your neighborhood, or one that's in a neighborhood you like to visit. Decide to patronize a small one instead of the big ones you've visited in the past. Follow an itinerant company like Theater Latté Da, Frank Theatre, or Walking Shadow Theatre Company, and you'll find yourself experiencing performances in different venues around town. Or, perhaps best of all, choose to support one based on their mission. Look at their websites: What is their intention? Do you share the same beliefs these theater artists are using to drive their creative work? Get on board.

- See a show more than once, preferably once early in the run and once near the close. On your first visit, pick out something that you particularly enjoy and something that you particularly question. Those are the things to watch closely when you return. Bonus points if your second visit is on a talkback performance, so you can start your question by saying, "This is the second time I've seen the show, and I've been wondering . . ." The company will love it.

- See the same title done by two different theater companies. You'll find the differences mind-boggling. How can they start with the same words and end up in such different places?

- Find a pal to go with regularly. Maybe choose one with different tastes who might take you to places and performances you
  wouldn't otherwise experience. If you are flush, buy an extra
  ticket each time you find something that interests you, and
  experiment with different friends until you find the right combination of interest, flexibility, and wit. Better yet, use that extra
  ticket for a young person of your acquaintance. You may not be
  assured of interest, at least at first, but you can certainly count
  on an unfiltered and frank assessment of the show. And you just
  might ignite a life's passion.
- Become a regular at a presenting venue; that is, choose a venue
  and not a company. In these cases, the leaders of the venue are
  doing the curating for your personal theater series; think variety.
  Try Bedlam Theatre in St. Paul's Lowertown, or Bryant-Lake
  Bowl in Minneapolis. In 2014, the Southern Theater launched
  an experimental performance membership program in which
  a monthly fee admits you to any and all performances by their
  member companies, more than a dozen at this writing.
- Go low or go for free. Check theaters for pay-what-you-can nights.
  Take a look at Mixed Blood's Radical Hospitality, which provides
  no-cost access to all productions for any audience member. Volunteer to usher in exchange for free seats. Patronize the theater work
  of colleges and universities, where ticket prices are low, enthusiasm
  is high, and bright new talent can be seen; these shows are sometimes directed or designed by the same artists who are freelancing
  in professional theaters all over town. Become a regular at the Playwrights' Center, where all admissions are free and you see skilled
  performers in new scripts in development. At Theater Latté Da, try
  the series NEXT: New Musicals in the Making, or the Rough Cuts
  series at Nautilus Music-Theater in St. Paul.
- Do some light research. Go to Minnesota Playlist (www
  .minnesotaplaylist.com) and read blog posts by theater people
  about community topics and issues. Read the Artscape column
  on MinnPost (www.minnpost.com/artscape) for recommenda-

tions and information on interesting projects coming up. Read the critics, print and online, and see if you agree with them. Like the theaters on Facebook to receive their postings, announcements, and review materials. Read the list of past winners of the Ivey Awards.

- When you get to the theater, read the program with special attention to the artist bios. You'll get to know these people, and you might find someone new to follow. When you get home, throw those programs into a box. In future weeks or months, you might wonder who that actor was in Play X playing the sweet young lover back in October. Could it possibly be the same person as the sinister murderer in Play Y you saw in February?

- For a little research and an enjoyable evening with friends, read the play aloud in advance of seeing it, particularly if it's Shakespeare. Really. If you organize, you get to choose the role you'll read—Hero or villain? Queen or saucy shepherdess? Soldier? Clown? Have no fear; create a judgment-free zone in your living room and go at it with gusto. Having spoken the lines in advance will exponentially increase your enjoyment of the performance.

- Inquire at the box office, or read website calendars, then stay for post-show talkbacks (some theaters use the term *discussion*), when the actors and artists come out to the stage and sit down to talk about the show and field your questions. Move down front. Ask a question. Always start by saying, "I love your work. . . ."

- Go out after the show and talk about it; the babysitter can wait another hour. What did you like? What did you hate? Why did they do this or that? Post-show conversation is built into the Fringe Festival experience, says executive director Jeff Larson. He says, "What you want is the kind of work that you'll talk about at the bar afterward. The fantastic and the terrible really stick with you, and you cannot wait to get to the bar and say, 'Did you see that?!' We tell the artists to invite your audience to meet you at the bar; the bar is just as important to the festival as any of the art is."

• • •

Art is perilous. Every once in a while, the combined efforts of all the talent and aspirations of the artists are not successful. The show does not, as they say, reach its potential; sometimes it flat fails.

When your attention wanders and you're checking your watch, do not despair. The theater is complex. There is always, always something to watch. Look closely.

- When the leading character is down front and center delivering a speech, that means the audience is supposed to be watching her; everything on the stage is aimed to focus attention on her. If you're just not interested, change your focus. Watch the supporting characters, standing about elsewhere on the stage, or the extras filling in the corners of the picture. What are they doing at this moment? Those people have heard this speech dozens or hundreds of times before. They know the focus is not on them and won't be for a few more minutes; what are they doing in the meantime? Look carefully at their faces.
- Deploy your program information. Take a look at that leading character. Are the roles listed in her bio similar to the one you see her playing now, or different? Does she look the same on stage as in her program head shot? Would you know her on the street or in the grocery store?
- If an actor is playing more than one role, track her changes as she appears and reappears. Is her physical attitude different? Her voice? Did she change costumes or wigs before she reappeared from offstage?
- If an understudy was announced for this performance, focus on him or her. How is he or she doing?
- If there is live music and you can see the musicians, watch what they're doing. Is there a conductor? How can the actors see him? Can you guess why this particular choice of instruments?
- If there are dance numbers, try to guess which dancer is the choreographer, who created the dances, or dance captain, the person responsible for maintaining them as intended.

- Try focusing on some aspect of the designers' work. Listen for sound; what is its function during the show? How does the lighting create different moods to match particular scenes? Look at the costumes: How much work went into building that ball gown? Or that bathrobe? Or that beading?
- Look for the changes that happen on stage during intermission. Is anyone coming out, perhaps a stagehand dressed in black, to change props, or sweep up the snowfall, or move a table? Are there scene changes? Are they *au vista* (in sight), or in a blackout, or behind a curtain? Are the changes quick and smooth? Are they choreographed? Are they performed by stagehands? If actors are involved, are they moving that table or those chairs in character?

There is always, always something to watch; there are a million ways in. Welcome to the theater. It is "preposterous and sentimental," as actor Hume Cronyn once said. It's also profound and paltry, and inescapably human.

The show programs at Ten Thousand Things include performers' answers to the question "Why do theater?" Anna Sundberg, who played Juliet in their *Romeo and Juliet,* answered this way: "Theater teaches me empathy. It gives me much-needed mercy and communion. Theater does not turn away or judge in the face of humanity's ugliest revelations. It deepens my understanding of the world I live in and the people I meet. It is my constant instructor in what it is to be human." I agree.

Welcome to the theater. Please take your seat.

Biographies of Contributors

Lou Bellamy

An Obie Award–winning director, actor, and scholar, Lou Bellamy is the founder and co–artistic director of Penumbra Theatre, founded in 1976, an important artistic home for playwright August Wilson and renowned African American theater. A University of Minnesota faculty member for more than thirty years, Bellamy shares the helm at Penumbra with his daughter, Sarah Bellamy, who is slated to take over leadership upon his retirement.

Sarah Bellamy

Sarah Bellamy is a playwright, director, and educator and serves as co–artistic director at Penumbra Theatre alongside her father and Penumbra's founder, Lou Bellamy. A regarded scholar and Minneapolis native, Bellamy has been leading racial equality and social justice efforts within the field and deepening community engagement as central to the work of Penumbra. She serves on the board of directors of Theatre Communications Group as the co–vice chair and also chairs the Equity, Diversity, and Inclusion Committee. In 2015 Bellamy was named a Bush Fellow.

Sonya Berlovitz

Sonya Berlovitz is a costume and textile designer. Between 1980 and 2008, Berlovitz designed more than fifty productions for Theatre de la Jeune Lune. She has designed for numerous other local companies, including the Moving Company, the Children's Theatre Company, the Guthrie Theater, the Jungle Theater, and Ten Thousand Things, as well as for companies across the country. Her work has been honored domestically and internationally, including being chosen for exhibition at the 2007 and 2011 Prague Quadrennials. In 2014 Berlovitz's costume designs were selected for a show at the Bakhrushin Museum of Theater Design in Moscow.

Bain Boehlke

A Minnesota native, Bain Boehlke has been a fixture of Twin Cities theater for more than fifty years as an actor, director, set designer, writer, and producer. Founder of the Jungle Theater, Boehlke retired from his position as artistic director in June 2015 after twenty-five years at the helm. He was awarded the 2009 McKnight Foundation Distinguished Artist Award and the 2011 Ivey Award for Lifetime Achievement.

Peter Brosius

Peter Brosius is the artistic director of the Children's Theatre Company, a position he has held since 1997. The work of CTC has been repeatedly honored under his leadership, including with a Tony Award for Sustained Excellence, and Brosius has supported new play development and educational initiatives such as the acclaimed Neighborhood Bridges program. Prior to his appointment at CTC, Brosius directed new and established works across the country and was the artistic director of the Honolulu Theatre for Youth, a staff director at the Mark Taper Forum, and a director at the Sundance Playwrights Laboratory. He has been honored with the Theatre Communications Group's Alan Schneider Director Award as well as by the Los Angeles Drama Critics Circle and the Ivey Awards.

Carlyle Brown

Carlyle Brown is a Minneapolis-based writer, producer, and performer. A recipient of numerous commissions, fellowships, and residencies, Brown is the founder and artistic director of Carlyle Brown & Company. He is also a core writer of the Playwrights' Center and has worked as an educator and theater artist across the nation.

Chris A. Code

Chris A. Code is a longtime stage manager at the Guthrie Theater. He has shepherded more than sixty productions on the Guthrie's stages.

Jesse Cogswell

Jesse Cogswell is a 2013 University of Minnesota graduate with an MFA in lighting design and technology. Cogswell has worked as a designer, programmer, and master electrician for a number of local institutions.

Jeremy Cohen

Since 2010 Jeremy Cohen has been the producing artistic director at the Playwrights' Center, the nation's preeminent organization supporting playwrights and promoting new works. Formerly he served as the associate artistic director and director of new play development at Hartford Stage. He served as founding artistic director of Naked Eye Theatre Company in Chicago. Cohen is experienced in new play development and premieres and has earned numerous directing awards.

Richard Cohen

Minnesota state senator Richard Cohen, chairman of the senate finance committee, is known for his advocacy for arts funding. A longtime advocate for increased support of the Minnesota State Arts Board and regional arts councils, he created and facilitated the Minnesota Legacy Amendment, which, beginning in 2008, provides twenty-five years of consistent public support for the arts. The originator of the St. Paul Cultural STAR program, which provides arts and cultural funding within the capital city, Cohen additionally serves on the board of directors for both the Guthrie Theater and the Saint Paul Chamber Orchestra. He has been honored by Americans for the Arts with the National Leadership Award and was appointed to the President's Committee on the Arts and Humanities by President Barack Obama in 2009.

Richard Cook

Richard Cook is the artistic director of Park Square Theatre. In 2011 he launched the Artistic Associates program. Cook led the theater's expansion to a second stage in 2014 and announced production collaborations with Theatre Pro Rata, Girl Friday Productions, and Sandbox Theatre, housed on Park Square's Andy Boss Thrust Stage.

Marcus Dilliard

Marcus Dilliard has designed the lighting for many productions at the Guthrie Theater, Theatre de la Jeune Lune, the Minnesota Opera, the Children's Theatre Company, and dozens of regional companies across the country. His work has earned many fellowships and awards. He is the chair of the University of Minnesota's Department of Theatre Arts and Dance.

Teresa Eyring

Teresa Eyring was appointed executive director of the Theatre Communications Group, the national organization for professional nonprofit American theater, in 2007, and she has overseen the implementation of a new strategic plan focusing on equity, diversity, and inclusion as well as on audience and community engagement. Past executive positions include managing director at the Children's Theatre Company and assistant executive director at the Guthrie Theater. Eyring serves on the board of directors of the Performing Arts Alliance and the Actors Fund. She was honored with the 2015 Distinguished Achievement Award in Management by the trade organization United States Institute for Theatre Technology (USITT).

Barbara Field

Barbara Field is a playwright and founding member of the Playwrights' Center. Her adaptations and original works have been seen across the country. Field has been honored with numerous fellowships and served as the playwright-in-residence at the Guthrie Theater from 1974 to 1981. Her book *New Classics from the Guthrie Theater: Classical Adaptations for the American Stage* was published in 2003; two volumes of her own collected plays have also been published, in 2011 and 2014.

Nathaniel Fuller

Nathaniel Fuller debuted on the Guthrie stage in January 1988 and has performed in every season since then, appearing in more than eighty productions. He has performed at many other Twin Cities theaters as well. He resides in Minneapolis with his wife, actress Cathleen Fuller.

Bradley Greenwald

Bradley Greenwald is an actor, singer, and writer with twenty-five years of full-time freelancing in the Twin Cities. Known for his leading roles with prestigious local institutions, he has received several awards, including a Minnesota State Arts Board fellowship in music, a McKnight Theater Artist fellowship, and a 2006 Ivey Award. Greenwald adapted the novel *A Wrinkle in Time* into a libretto for Libby Larsen's opera.

Rich Hamson

Rich Hamson is the costume designer and costume shop manager for Chanhassen Dinner Theatres, for which he has designed more than twenty-five productions. His designs have been seen on national tours and on stage at renowned regional theaters, including the Guthrie Theater, the Minnesota Opera, the Children's Theatre Company, and the Ordway Center for the Performing Arts, as well as with various midsize companies and educational institutions throughout the state. He has been repeatedly honored for his contributions to theater artistry in the Twin Cities, most recently as *Lavender Magazine*'s Theater Artist of the Year and Best Large Theater Costume Designer in 2014.

H. Adam Harris

H. Adam Harris is an actor and teaching artist. A Detroit native, Harris is a graduate of the University of Minnesota/Guthrie Theater BFA Actor Training Program. He is a member of the Ten Thousand Things Artist Core, a teaching artist with the Guthrie Theater, a faculty member of the Saint Paul Conservatory for Performing Artists, and the teen programs coordinator of Penumbra Theatre Company, in addition to his onstage appearances in those and other local institutions.

Michelle Hensley

The founder of Ten Thousand Things Theater, Michelle Hensley has directed and produced more than fifty tours presented to low-income audiences, with most shows making local critics' top ten lists. The Public Theater in New York, the California Shakespeare Theater, and San Diego's Old Globe have all adopted TTT's touring model. Named Best Artistic Director by the *Star Tribune* in 2012, Hensley also received the Francesca Primus Prize for outstanding contribution to the theater by an emerging female artist. The Minnesota Historical Society Press published her book about Ten Thousand Things, *All the Lights On*, in 2015.

Aditi Brennan Kapil

Aditi Brennan Kapil is a playwright, actress, and director. A Macalester graduate and Minneapolis resident, Kapil is of Bulgarian and Indian descent and grew up in Stockholm, Sweden. She serves as playwright-in-residence at Mixed Blood Theatre, as an artistic associate at Park Square Theatre, and as core writer at the Playwrights' Center. Kapil was named Artist of the Year by *City Pages* in 2013.

Kevin Kling

Kevin Kling is an acclaimed playwright and storyteller as well as a commentator for National Public Radio's *All Things Considered*. A native of Osseo and a Minneapolis resident, Kling has been recognized for his artistry by the National Endowment for the Arts, the McKnight Foundation, the Minnesota State Arts Board, the Bush Foundation, the Jerome Foundation, and others.

Jeff Larson

Jeff Larson was appointed executive director of the Minnesota Fringe Festival in 2013 after more than sixteen years in various roles at the organization. A graduate of the University of Minnesota Theatre Arts and Dance Department and the Carlson School of Management, Larson has worked as a director and lighting designer at numerous regional institutions in addition to his tenure at the Fringe.

C. Andrew Mayer

C. Andrew Mayer is a Minneapolis native. His work in the theater began when he graduated from the Children's Theatre Company and School, and it continues to this day. Mayer has worked with several local institutions, including the History Theatre, the Jungle Theater, Mixed Blood, Park Square, Pillsbury House, the Minnesota Opera, and the Guthrie. He has been honored with a Playwrights' Center McKnight Theatre Artist fellowship and an AUDELCO Award.

Tyler Michaels

Tyler Michaels is a Minneapolis-based performer, improviser, and director. A founding member of Bearded Men Improv, Michaels has performed with the Guthrie Theater, the Children's Theatre Company, Hennepin Theatre Trust, and Theater Latté Da, among many others. He was named Best Actor by *Minnesota Monthly* and Minneapolis's Best Actor in a Musical by Broadwayworld.com. In 2014 he was honored with the Emerging Artist Ivey Award.

John Miller-Stephany

John Miller-Stephany was artistic administrator at the Guthrie Theater from 1996 to 1999 and then from 1999 to 2015 served as associate artistic director, responsible for coordinating casting for all Guthrie productions. During his staff tenure, Miller-Stephany directed sixteen acclaimed productions at the Guthrie. He has also been a guest director for other resident theaters, including companies in both Minneapolis and St. Paul.

Bonnie Morris

Bonnie Morris is the producing director at Illusion Theater, where she has worked as an actor, writer, educator, and producer since its founding in 1974. Passionate about new work and artists, Morris has co-authored all of Illusion's educational plays. In 2014 she was honored alongside Michael Robins with the Ivey Award for Lifetime Achievement.

Kira Obolensky

Kira Obolensky is an award-winning playwright and writer based in Minneapolis. A 2013–16 Mellon Foundation playwright-in-residence fellow at Ten Thousand Things, Obolensky teaches playwriting at the University of Minnesota and is a member of the dramatic writing faculty at Spalding University's MFA Program for Writers.

Ron Peluso

Ron Peluso became the artistic director of the History Theatre in 1995. He has commissioned more than seventy playwrights and composers and has produced more than sixty original works, including *Sisters of Swing* and *Beyond the Rainbow*, which have played in dozens of regional theaters. He has directed more than 160 professional productions with such companies as Florida Stage, Riverside Theatre, Pennsylvania Opera Theater, Mixed Blood Theatre, and the Minnesota Opera. Peluso holds an MFA in directing from the University of Minnesota and is married to actress Sue Scott.

T. Mychael Rambo

T. Mychael Rambo is an actor, vocalist, and educator. A member of the Penumbra Theatre Company, Rambo is an adjunct professor for the Theatre Arts and Dance Department at the University of Minnesota. He has performed with such local theaters as the Guthrie Theater, Illusion Theater, Mixed Blood Theatre, and the Children's Theatre Company, and he has participated in several national and regional tours and international performances. As an artistic producer, he has collaborated with Minnesota Public Radio and presented work at Target Center. In addition to television appearances and work as a jazz vocalist, Rambo has received numerous awards for artistic excellence as a musician and actor.

Jack Reuler

Jack Reuler is a mainstay of Twin Cities theater, nationally recognized for his commitment to successful pluralism, individual equality, and racial equity as founder and artistic director of the Mixed Blood Theatre. Reuler is the originator of the groundbreaking Radical Hospitality program, providing no-cost and barrier-free admission to any audience member. In 2006 he was honored with the Ivey's Lifetime Achievement Award.

Randy Reyes

Randy Reyes succeeded Rick Shiomi as artistic director of Mu Performing Arts in 2013. Reyes is a Los Angeles native, was trained at the University of Utah and Juilliard, and is renowned as an actor and director. He has performed with numerous local institutions including the Guthrie Theater, Mu Performing Arts, Ten Thousand Things, and Workhaus Collective.

Michael Robins

Michael Robins is the founder and executive producing director at Illusion Theater. Since 1974 he has guided nearly 350 plays to production. In 2014 Robins was honored alongside Bonnie Morris with the Ivey Award for Lifetime Achievement.

Peter Rothstein

Peter Rothstein is the founding artistic director of Theater Latté Da and a renowned director of theater, musical theater, opera, and new work development. He was named one of Minnesota's Artists of the Year by the *Star Tribune* in 2001, 2007, and 2011; Theater Artist of the Year by *Lavender Magazine* in 2010; Best Director of the Year by *City Pages* in 2006 and 2010; and Artist of the Year by *City Pages* in 2012. He has also received six Ivey Awards for Overall Excellence. Rothstein serves on the board of directors for the National Alliance for Musical Theatre, Alive and Kickin', and the Twin Cities' Ivey Awards. He is the creator of *All Is Calm: The Christmas Truce of 1914* and *Steerage Song*.

Joel Sass

Director and designer Joel Sass is highly regarded both locally and nationally. Born in Wisconsin and based in Minneapolis, he is known for his imaginative, visually playful style. Sass has worked with numerous institutions including the Jungle Theater, the Guthrie Theater, Park Square Theatre, and national Shakespeare festivals. From 1994 to 2003, Sass spearheaded the Mary Worth Theatre Company. He has received multiple awards and honors, including being named Best Designer Minneapolis in 2013 by *City Pages*.

Rick Shiomi

Rick Shiomi is a playwright, stage director, and taiko artist. He first came to Minnesota as a visiting speaker following the success of his first play, *Yellow Fever*, in San Francisco and New York. He is the former artistic director and a cofounder of Mu Performing Arts. Shiomi also spearheaded the formation of Mu Daiko, a taiko drumming ensemble, for which he was lead player and composer for thirteen years before stepping aside in 2010. He is the recipient of numerous national and local awards for his work as a playwright, composer, and cultural leader; he received the Ivey Award for Lifetime Achievement in 2012.

Anna Sundberg

Anna Sundberg is an actress and performer. Since moving to the Twin Cities in 2006, Sundberg has acted with several respected local institutions, including the Guthrie Theater, the Children's Theatre Company, the Jungle Theater, Ten Thousand Things, and many more. She has received multiple awards and was named 2013's Best Actor Under 30 by the *Star Tribune*.

Kate Sutton-Johnson

Kate Sutton-Johnson is a freelance set designer specializing in environmental and stage design for the theater as well as for museum exhibits, corporate events, and trade shows. She has worked with the Children's Theatre Company, the Ordway Center for the Performing Arts, the Guthrie Theater, Mixed Blood Theatre, and Park Square Theatre, among others. Sutton-Johnson received the 2007 Emerging Artist Ivey Award and, along with the full artistic team, the 2014 Ivey Award for *Cabaret*, produced by Theater Latté Da and Hennepin Theatre Trust.

Christine Tschida

Christine Tschida is the director of Northrop, the center for the arts, performance, and academics at the University of Minnesota. She was formerly an agent for American and international dance and theater companies. She spent eleven years as producer of Garrison Keillor's *A Prairie Home Companion*. She served as a line producer at the Brooklyn Academy of Music and also as director of special projects for the Kennedy Center's American National Theater. Her touring experience began at the Guthrie Theater, where, as director of outreach programs, she booked and managed the largest national tour that theater had ever undertaken.

Ricardo Vazquez

Ricardo Vazquez is an actor and writer who has performed with Mixed Blood Theatre, Park Square Theatre, Ten Thousand Things, the History Theatre, Pangea World Theater, and Teatro del Pueblo. He has also appeared in local and national commercials and on the syndicated television show *M@dAbout*. An alumnus of the University of Minnesota/Guthrie Theater BFA Actor Training Program, Vazquez received the 2012 Many Voices Playwright Fellowship and has written for Minnesotaplaylist.com, Minneapolis One-Minute Play Festival, and the University of Minnesota New Works series. In 2013 he was honored with the Emerging Artist Ivey Award.

Sally Wingert

Sally Wingert is a leading performer in Twin Cities theater. An original company member for Garland Wright, Wingert has performed in more than eighty productions at the Guthrie Theater since 1985 and graced the stages of other local institutions, including Mixed Blood Theatre, the Minnesota Jewish Theatre Company, Ten Thousand Things, and Theater Latté Da. Repeatedly lauded and honored for her work, Wingert was named Artist of the Year by the *Star Tribune* in 2013 and Best Actress in Minneapolis 2014 by *City Pages* and was recognized for four separate performances at the 2014 Ivey Awards.

Fifty-five Theaters in the Twin Cities Metro

The Twin Cities theater scene is constantly growing and changing. This list concentrates on professional companies that present regular performances and, with a few exceptions, are located in the core of the Twin Cities. There are others aplenty. Descriptive notes are largely taken from the theaters' own websites.

Artistry
artistrymn.org, Bloomington

"Artistry serves audiences and artists by producing theater, exhibitions, and arts education opportunities at the Bloomington Center for the Arts and other locations throughout the Twin Cities."

Bedlam Theatre
bedlamtheatre.org, Lowertown, St. Paul

"Bedlam Theatre's mission is to produce radical works of theatre with a focus on collaboration and a unique blend of professional and community art. Bedlam builds culture through and around experimental performing arts—and their audiences. Bedlam supports artists that challenge not just form and content, but process as well on their adventure to reflect, celebrate, and reinvent themselves and their society. Fun, wild, anything-is-possible theater is our passion."

Brave New Workshop
www.bravenewworkshop.com, Downtown Minneapolis

"Crafting audacious, hilarious, and thought-provoking original comedy, improv, and satire in Minneapolis since 1958, the Brave New Workshop Comedy Theatre is a Twin Cities comedy institution, and a truly unique place to laugh, learn, think, and play."

Bryant-Lake Bowl Theater

www.bryantlakebowl.com, South Minneapolis

"A combination bowling alley/restaurant/bar/theater offering food, alcohol, and live performance."

Chanhassen Dinner Theatres

www.chanhassentheatres.com, Chanhassen

"Chanhassen Dinner Theatres is committed to delighting its audiences and creating lifelong memories with a high-quality end-to-end theatre, dining, and service experience."

Children's Theatre Company

www.childrenstheatre.org, South Minneapolis

"Children's Theatre Company creates extraordinary theatre experiences that educate, challenge and inspire young people and their communities. We are the leaders in engaging our community and our country in the power of theatre to enrich and transform the lives of young people."

Dark & Stormy Productions

www.darkstormy.org, various locations

"Dark & Stormy Productions seeks to enrich the community by providing artistically excellent, relevant, and thought-provoking professional productions that engage and inspire both the audience and the artist."

Four Humors Theater

www.fourhumorstheater.com, various locations

"Four Humors strives to create art that celebrates the humor, stupidity, and beauty of our world by letting the artist connect with the audience in a vulnerable and honest way."

Frank Theatre

www.franktheatre.org, various locations

"Frank Theatre is a professional theatre company committed to producing unique work that stretches the skills of the artists who create the work while simultaneously challenging the everyday perceptions of the audience through the exploration of ideas and issues of social, political and/or cultural concern."

Girl Friday Productions

www.girlfridayproductions.org, various locations

"Girl Friday Productions' mission is to nurture artists, inspire audiences, and illuminate the human condition."

Gremlin Theatre

www.gremlin-theatre.org, Minneapolis

"Gremlin Theatre seeks to provide artistically brilliant, accessible, and enjoyable theatrical experiences for the Twin Cities community, perpetuating the idea of theatre as a relevant, entertaining, and socially valuable activity for the audience and the artist."

The Guthrie Theater

www.guthrietheater.org, Minneapolis

"The Guthrie Theater, founded in 1963, is an American center for theater performance, production, education and professional training. By presenting both classical literature and new work from diverse cultures, the Guthrie illuminates the common humanity connecting Minnesota to the peoples of the world."

History Theatre
www.historytheatre.com, Downtown St. Paul

"History Theatre entertains, educates, and inspires through creating, developing, and producing new and existing works that explore Minnesota's past and the diverse American experience. Its work provides a unique lens which links our past to the present, explores our common heritage, and illuminates our understanding of what it means to be American."

Illusion Theater
www.illusiontheater.org, Downtown Minneapolis

"Illusion Theater's mission is to create theater that illuminates the illusions, myths and realities of our times and to catalyze personal and social change."

Interact
interactcenter.com, St. Paul

"Interact's mission to create art that challenges perceptions of disability has opened doors for artists with disabilities and audiences eager to experience their work, who might never have seen the arts as a life choice, but who now see the arts as essential to their humanity. Interact is multi-cultural, intergenerational, and embraces the entire spectrum of disability labels."

In the Heart of the Beast Puppet and Mask Theatre
hobt.org, South Minneapolis

"HOBT uses water, flour, newspaper, paint and unlimited imagination to tell stories that explore the struggles and celebrations of human existence. Drawing inspiration from the world's traditions of puppet and mask theater and its lively roots in transformative ritual and street theater, HOBT creates vital, poetic theater for all ages and backgrounds, bringing people together for the common good."

Jungle Theater

www.jungletheater.com, South Minneapolis

"The Jungle Theater creates dynamic, world-class theater, bringing an artistic depth and poetic fire to plays drawn from our rich theatrical heritage as well as from the body of work written in our own time. The Jungle aspires to create definitive productions that engender an intimate yet powerful relationship between actor and audience, transforming lives with the undeniable magic of the living theater as well as enriching its role as an active and catalytic partner in the cultural and economic life of the neighborhood in which it resides."

Live Action Set

liveactionset.org, various locations

"Live Action Set is committed to creating visually poetic, wildly imaginative, and accessible performance experiences that harness the indefinable power of the human spirit. Live Action Set's ensemble-driven work dissolves artistic boundaries, pursues issues of essential value to its audiences, and engages people and communities in profound relationships."

Minneapolis Musical Theatre

aboutmmt.org, Downtown Minneapolis

"The Minneapolis Musical Theatre is dedicated to providing community access to high quality yet affordable works of music theatre never before— or very rarely—seen by Twin City audiences."

Minnesota Fringe Festival

www.fringefestival.org, various locations

"The mission of Minnesota Fringe Festival is to connect adventurous artists with adventurous audiences by creating open, supportive forums for free and diverse artistic expression. Minnesota Fringe does not jury, judge or censor the work of any artist and returns a majority of the box office to the artists."

Minnesota Jewish Theatre Company
mnjewishtheatre.org, St. Paul

"Minnesota Jewish Theatre Company ignites the hearts and minds of all people of all cultural backgrounds by producing theater of the highest artistic standards. Rooted in Jewish content, our work explores differences, illuminates commonalities, and fosters greater understanding among all people."

Mixed Blood Theatre Company
www.mixedblood.com, West Bank Minneapolis

"Mixed Blood Theatre, a professional, multi-racial company, promotes cultural pluralism and individual equality through artistic excellence, using theater to address artificial barriers that keep people from succeeding in American society. Its vision is to be the definitive destination where theater artists and audiences representing the global village can create and share work that spawns a ripple effect of social change and revolutionizes access to theater."

The Moving Company
themovingco.org, various locations

"Based in Minneapolis, The Moving Company was founded in 2008, and is dedicated to creating new works of theatre for audiences locally, nationally and throughout the world, and to a collaborative process that nurtures and empowers the creativity of all artists. Our mission is to create and produce new and challenging theatre that builds on the past, is grounded in the present and looks to the future, as well as to maintain and nourish an atmosphere for the development of new ideas."

Mu Performing Arts

www.muperformingarts.org, various locations

"Mu produces great performances born of arts, equity, and justice from the heart of the Asian American experience. It is a mission born of two needs; the need to gain due recognition as Asian Americans in 21st century America, and the need to facilitate a clearer understanding of our identity and responsibilities within our own diverse community. Through this artistic work, Mu seeks to communicate the Asian American experience as a unique American story with universally relevant themes for all audiences."

Nautilus Music-Theater

www.nautilusmusictheater.org, various locations

"Since 1986 Nautilus, formerly The New Music-Theater Ensemble, has been dedicated to the development of new operas and other forms of music-theater, along with innovative productions of existing work. We provide opportunities for the professional growth of music-theater artists who create, develop, and produce work that is emotionally expansive, dramatically engaging, and spiritually stimulating."

Off-Leash Area: Contemporary Performance Works

www.offleasharea.org, various locations

"Off-Leash Area was founded in Minneapolis in 1999 and creates original interdisciplinary performance work. Named after the public parks where dogs run untethered, OLA's creative approach is likewise playful, crosses boundaries, and takes risks. OLA is committed to uphold the transformative power of the live performance experience, trusting in the intelligence and capability of its audience to follow them on each new journey of the imagination. If there is any one theme that runs through all our work it is a belief in the resilience of the individual human spirit as it seeks to achieve growth and fulfillment in the face of personal and societal barriers."

Old Log Theatre
www.oldlog.com, Excelsior

"The Old Log presents musical, contemporary, classic and family theatre. Established in 1940, Old Log Theatre is the oldest professional theater in the state of Minnesota."

Open Eye Figure Theatre
www.openeyetheatre.org, South Minneapolis

"Open Eye Figure Theatre creates original figure theatre, animating the inanimate on an intimate, human scale, trains the next generation of figure theatre artists, and advances adventurous, artist-driven programming. Nationally recognized for bringing a visual feast of evocative figure theater to the stage, the company's whimsical yet profound work surprises and delights whether experienced in the historic jewel box theater in Minneapolis or in neighborhoods throughout the Twin Cities with the Driveway Tour. From experimental object works to puppet shows in backyards to community pageants to miniature spectacles, Open Eye consistently creates a unique, contagious exchange between artists and audiences."

Pangea World Theater
www.pangeaworldtheater.org, various locations

"Pangea World Theater is a progressive space for transformation in which conversations about race, gender, ethnicity, human rights, politics and social justice form an important backbone for our work. We collaborate with award winning international artists and companies to create plays and performances that speak across geography and culture. Pangea World Theater illuminates the human condition, celebrates cultural differences, and promotes human rights by creating and presenting international, multi-disciplinary theater."

Park Square Theatre

parksquaretheatre.org, Downtown St. Paul

"Park Square Theatre seeks to enrich our community by producing and presenting exceptional live theatre that touches the heart, engages the mind, and delights the spirit. Located in the Historic Hamm Building, Park Square Theatre opened an additional venue, the Andy Boss Thrust Stage, in 2014."

Penumbra Theatre

penumbratheatre.org, St. Paul

"Penumbra Theatre creates professional productions that are artistically excellent, thought provoking, relevant, and illuminate the human condition through the prism of the African American experience."

Pillsbury House Theatre

pillsburyhouseandtheatre.org, South Minneapolis

"Pillsbury House Theatre's mission is to create challenging theatre to inspire choice, change and connection. Through the mainstage season and other programming, Pillsbury House Theatre illuminates the differences that make each person unique and the similarities that bring people together, within an artistic environment that promotes understanding and leads to positive action."

Playwrights' Center

pwcenter.org, Minneapolis

"The Playwrights' Center champions playwrights and new plays to build upon a living theater that demands new and innovative works. Founded in 1971 by five writers seeking artistic and professional support, the Playwrights' Center today serves more playwrights in more ways than any other organization in the country."

Plymouth Playhouse

plymouthplayhouse.com, Plymouth

"Dedicated to fostering new Off-Broadway style American musical comedies."

Red Eye Theater

www.redeyetheater.org, Minneapolis

"Innovative, experimental, spirited, distinctive, startling, daring and out of the ordinary, Red Eye is a multi-disciplinary creative laboratory that supports the development and production of pioneering theater performance work. In addition to creating its own acclaimed multimedia theatrical productions, Red Eye functions as an incubator and producer of other artists' works."

Sandbox Theatre

www.sandboxtheatreonline.com, St. Paul

"Driven by the collaborative spirit to create new and newly-imagined performance artworks, and to foster the development of artists."

Savage Umbrella

www.savageumbrella.org, St. Paul

"Savage Umbrella co-operates as a company to create new works of theater, constantly striving to engage artists and audiences in vital discourse. We believe theater is critical shelter, embodying compassionate space for relevant conversation."

7th House Theater

www.7thhousetheater.org, various locations

"7th House Theater is dedicated to creating new, innovative, and reimagined stage-productions with an emphasis on music as a theatrical element. Founded in 2013, 7th House seeks to get at the heart of the plays we produce by stripping them down to their bare essentials. Our aesthetic is minimal, and focuses our productions on the connection between actors, musicians, and audience."

The Southern Theater
southerntheater.org, West Bank, Minneapolis

"The Southern Theater, one of the Twin Cities' oldest performance venues, fosters a community of exceptional artists through their ARTshare residency program, giving audience members unlimited access for a low monthly fee."

Stages Theatre Company
stagestheatre.org, Hopkins

"Stages Theatre Company is committed to the enrichment and education of children and youth in a professional theatre environment that stimulates artistic excellence and personal growth."

SteppingStone Theatre
www.steppingstonetheatre.org. St. Paul

"SteppingStone Theatre's mission is to develop the whole child by using educational theatre programs and fully-staged productions to build self-esteem, confidence, and a sense of community while celebrating diversity in a non-competitive environment. SteppingStone's programs foster creativity, self-expression, and self-confidence; nurture and showcase the creative potential of young people; stimulate creative thinking and expression; teach children and youth about history, diverse cultures, literature and the arts through engaging and entertaining learning; and help to create in youth a lifelong appreciation for the arts."

Teatro del Pueblo
teatrodelpueblo.org, St. Paul

"Teatro del Pueblo promotes Latino culture through the creation and presentation of performing arts. Teatro develops and supports Latino artists, provides educational opportunities for all to experience Latino culture, and promotes cross-cultural dialogue."

Ten Thousand Things

www.tenthousandthings.org, various locations

"Ten Thousand Things brings lively, intelligent theater to people with little access to the wealth of the arts, who in turn help us reimagine theater—invigorating ancient tales, classic stories, and contemporary plays through vital, open interactions between the region's finest actors and non-traditional audiences."

Theater Latté Da

www.theaterlatteda.com, various locations

"The mission of Theater Latté Da is to create new connections between story, music, artist and audience by exploring and expanding the art of musical theater. Founded in 1998, the company stands committed to a rigorous experimentation that expands the art form and speaks to a contemporary audience, challenging us to think deeply about the world in which we live."

Theatre Coup d'Etat

www.theatrecoupdetat.com, various locations

"Theatre Coup d'Etat's mission is to provoke an emotional and analytical response in our audiences by showing the depth of the human condition through both classical and contemporary works."

Theatre Forever

www.theatreforever.com, various locations

"Theatre Forever is a live performance company focused on the creation of new work. Since 2005, the company has created profoundly thought-provoking, delightfully playful, and accessible theatre and performance work through their unique collaborative and devising process. Theatre Forever is an ever-evolving ensemble of performers, writers, designers, and theatre-creators. Theatre Forever embraces the impulse to create the unforgettable and bring life to art that exists beyond ourselves"

Theatre Pro Rata
theatreprorata.org, various locations

"We are Pro Rata: we create smart, vivid, varied, and gutsy programming. As an audience member, you'll be part of moving, thought-provoking theatre. Our mission is to each of us: a foundation in the play, a pursuit of creative excellence, and a continuation of curiosity."

Theatre Unbound
theatreunbound.com, various locations

"Theatre Unbound delivers thought-provoking live theatre conceived and created by women, providing audiences with engaging, rarely-seen perspectives on issues that are relevant and universal."

TigerLion Arts
www.tigerlion.org, various locations

"TigerLion Arts is a Minneapolis-based production company. We celebrate human wisdom and the spirit of nature through creative works that awaken, inform, and delight."

Transatlantic Love Affair
transatlanticloveaffair.org, various locations

"A physical theatre ensemble. As an artistic community, we value the role of collaboration in the creation of original work; we commit ourselves to the imaginative re-telling of relevant stories; we believe the human body to be the ultimate theatrical instrument."

20% Theatre Company
www.tctwentypercent.org, various locations

"20% Theatre Company Twin Cities is committed to supporting and vigorously promoting the work of female and transgender theatre artists, and celebrating the unique contribution of these artists to social justice and human rights."

Urban Samurai Productions

www.urbansamurai.org, various locations

"The mission of Urban Samurai Productions is to provide Twin Cities artists and patrons access to cutting-edge theater by presenting original plays, rarely-produced works, or new perspectives on contemporary classics."

Walking Shadow Theatre Company

walkingshadowcompany.org, various locations

"Walking Shadow Theatre Company believes the human soul is a disturbing and beautiful place. We create engaging and memorable experiences that promote an exchange of ideas inspired by the stories we tell. Through new and established material, careful research, and bold artistic expression we develop high-quality theatre that illuminates the depths and heights of human capacity. We are dedicated to developing the talents of our artists, nurturing audience commitment to the arts, facilitating community dialogue, and examining local culture in a global context."

Workhaus Collective

workhauscollective.org, various locations

"Workhaus Collective creates a direct and immediate relationship between playwright and audience by fully producing original plays under the artistic leadership of the playwright. Our vision is to carve out a space in Minnesota, and nationally, for risky, new, text-based scripts created by Minnesota writers that all Minnesotans can enjoy and be proud of."

Yellow Tree Theatre

yellowtreetheatre.com, Osseo

"Yellow Tree Theatre brings stories to life that ignite passion, inspire laughter and awaken possibility while exploring and celebrating the great complexities of the human spirit. We strive to produce high-quality professional productions in the heart of the Northwest suburbs of Minneapolis, making live theatre more accessible to the community."

Index

Page numbers in *italics* indicate illustrations.

Image Details

page 59
Into the Woods: music and lyrics by
  Stephen Sondheim; book by James
  Lapine
Mu Performing Arts
Directed by Rick Shiomi
Music direction by Denise Prosek
Set by Gunther Gullickson
Costumes by Paula Lee
Lights by Karin Olson
Music Direction by Denise Prosek
Sound by Tom Sandelands

page 94
Oedipus El Rey by Luis Alfaro
Teatro del Pueblo and Pangea World
  Theater
Directed by Dipankar Mukherjee
Set by Karin Olson
Costumes by Jeff Stolz
Lights by Tom Mays

page 125
Big White Fog by Theodore Ward
Penumbra Theatre and the Guthrie
  Theater
Directed by Lou Bellamy
Set by Douglas Stein
Costumes by Paul Tazewell
Lights by Allen L. Hughes

page 128
Cabaret: book by Joe Masteroff, based
  on a book by Christopher Isherwood;
  music by John Kander; lyrics by Fred
  Ebb
Theater Latté Da
Directed by Peter Rothstein
Music direction by Denise Prosek
Choreographed by Michael Matthew
  Ferrell
Set by Kate Sutton-Johnson
Costumes by Rich Hamson
Lights by Marcus Dilliard

page 136
Robin Hood by Greg Banks
Children's Theatre Company
Directed by Greg Banks
Set by Joseph Stanley
Costumes by Mary Anna Culligan
Lights by Becky Fuller Jensen
Composer/Sound Design by Victor
  Zupanc

Peg Guilfoyle spent ten years as production stage manager and production manager for artistic directors Liviu Ciulei and Garland Wright at the Guthrie Theater. She has been the producing director for the Department of Theatre Arts and Dance at the University of Minnesota and managing director of the Minnesota Centennial Showboat on Harriet Island. She has been a freelance stage and production manager for the Ordway Center for the Performing Arts, Mixed Blood Theatre, Denver Center Theatre Company, Arizona Theatre Company, and Elitch Theatre Company star stock, and has consulted as an arts manager for the University of Minnesota.

She is the author of *The Guthrie Theater: Images, History and Inside Stories*, for which she won the Midwest Book Award, and other regional history books. Her company, Peg Projects, Inc., has produced histories for Camp du Nord YMCA, Northern Star Boy Scout Council, Gustavus Adolphus College, Plymouth Congregational Church, and the Basilica of Saint Mary; these books have won numerous awards, including the Minnesota Book Award.

Peg lives in downtown St. Paul with husband John Baillie, with whom she co-owns Cedar Pet Clinic Lake Elmo.

The author is available for readings, speaking engagements, and book clubs, and for book project consultations. Visit PegGuilfoyle.com for additional information.